Freedom

Reflections on a Fath   *...ship*

Freedom to Choose

Reflections on a Father/Son Relationship

ADESINA SULEIMAN

FM Publications

LONDON

Freedom to Choose: Reflections on a Father/Son Relationship
Text copyright © 2020 by Adesina Suleiman

FM Publications
ISBN: 978-1-9163938-0-6
FM Publications is a subsidiary of Fishers of Men Ministry

First edition published in London, United Kingdom in 2020 by FM Publications.
First printed in the United Kingdom in 2020.

All scripture quotations are taken from the New International Version of the Bible

www.fmministry.co.uk

Foreword

We are so excited about this book.

It is a very honest, insightful, heartfelt, readable, and helpful book. We are happy to recommend it to as many people as possible and hope you will too.

It is a book about the relationship between a father and his son, which also demonstrates the profound positive impact that reconciliation with our Heavenly Father, through repentance and faith in Jesus Christ, can have on key human relationships.

We have known Adesina for over eight years. What he has written genuinely reflects his character: he is honest, forthright, transparent, and fearlessly committed to serving our Lord, Jesus Christ. He is full of love and compassion for those who do not yet know Jesus as their Lord and Saviour and persistently participates in reaching such people, with engaging humility.

We hope and pray that, like us, you will be inspired and blessed by this book.

Tim & Pearl Akinluyi

Table of Contents

PROLOGUE

In this memoir, a personal narrative of my life is preceded by my account of my father's. It is therefore set out in two parts. The first is my reflection on my father's life and what I believe to be his journey to salvation. This story will comprise what I know about him, what I have heard said about him, and some assumptions about what I think might have happened. I will set out these sources of information and make them clear throughout the text.

The second part is a personal recount of my life up to the present moment. I have been prayerfully selective in what I have written about so that the purpose for which the book is written can be achieved. Again I will be sure to point out any assumptions or third party information that is used in the book.

I have deliberately removed details of people's names, locations, and other identifying details in order not to cause offence and also to protect the identity of some people who may not want to be recognisable. Locations are not particularly important to the book, especially as what I write about is not unique to any one nationality or culture. I have decided to keep my relative's true relationships as those are crucial to understanding the context of the story. Apart from the above, the book is a faithful account of the author's perspective and understanding.

This book comes under the Christian faith category. I write as a Christian, a child of God, and a Disciple of the Lord Jesus Christ. However, I aim to make this resource accessible to all people, whether they have faith in Jesus Christ or not, and so I have deliberately made it as easy to read as I can. A few terms that may not be widely understood are explained in the glossary.

The reason I have written this book is that I believe God wants me to use my life experience to encourage two specific groups of people. These groups form, in my opinion, the two groups in which the entire human race can be categorised. You are either like me, whom God has rescued from a dark place and has received the gift of eternal life; or you are like my earthly father who someone like me was earnestly praying to be saved. For those in the second category, it is important to add that even if everyone you know is of a different belief to Christianity, there are Christians unknown to you who are praying that everyone, including you, will receive the gift of salvation through Jesus Christ.

I believe the Holy Spirit gave me the title of this book, *Freedom to Choose*, many months before my father died. I knew I had to write a book with that title but I did not know when or how that was going to happen. God used the death of my father to give birth to the book. My hope and prayer for you as you read this is that God will use it to encourage you and bring forth a new beginning in you and that you will be able to exercise or continue to exercise your freedom to choose, as I have done.

PART ONE

My Father's Biography

According to available records, my father was born on 28th April 1930 in the suburbs of a major city in West Africa. His parents were from another town in the south-west of the country.

My father attended and completed his Standard 7 education and went on to achieve a Technical Certificate in Construction and Engineering. He was then sent by his parents to live with his uncle in another part of the country. It was to be there he started his family and spent most of his working life.

My father used to proudly state that he was a man of three places, born in one, raised in another and with heritage from a third via his parents. Another thing my father used to boast about was that he could speak the three main languages of the country plus a few other minor dialects.

My father started work as a Police Officer and later on went into a business partnership with his friend, starting a contracting firm. Later in life, he retired to the town where he was born, to lead the Islamic and Arabic School that was first established by his father, my grandfather. My father finally returned to where his parents were born and that was where he spent his final years.

Marrying more than one wife and inheriting wives from a late relative are allowed practices in both Islam and the West African culture my father lived. He was married to a total of four wives in his lifetime, although only two lived and gave birth to children for him. The second wife was his uncle's wife who he inherited when the uncle died. I did not hear much about that relationship and how it ended. The third wife was said to be a 'troublesome wife' who left very quickly after my father decided to marry a fourth wife. Apparently, the sole purpose of the fourth wife was to get rid of the third and by that account was a successful strategy!

So my father's main wives were his first (my mother) and the fourth, my step-mother. Together they gave birth to twelve surviving children, giving them a total of forty-eight grandchildren and eight great-grandchildren. I have heard about a couple of babies who died between my parents' first and second born. We also, unfortunately, lost my immediate younger brother at the age of 19.

Most people who knew my father would agree that he was a devoted man of God, a loving family man, an educator, very generous, and very funny. He was well travelled, easy-going, and able to interact with people of different ages, backgrounds, and religious belief systems. His loss weighs heavily on all those who knew him.

The Hope Of Salvation – What Are The Odds?

The bulk of this reflective account of my father's journey to salvation was written on Good Friday and Easter Monday in the year he died. On a personal level, this part of the journal is written based on the hope that one day my earthly father will be among the saints that will rise to meet with Jesus Christ on his second coming. But on a general level, the hope is that it will encourage others in a similar situation to mine or my late father's.

As the Bible puts it in 1 Thessalonians 4:16: 'for the Lord himself will come down from heaven, with a loud command, with the voice of the archangel and with the trumpet call of God, and the dead in Christ will rise first'.

My father's early life gave him nothing to suggest that he might find spiritual salvation in Christ. The odds were stacked against him as he was born in a town where they worship Satan. Yes, and I deliberately use the present tense because there are still people and homes in the area who worship the devil. The name of the compound[1] where he was born translates to 'the home where Satan was born' or an alternative translation as 'the home that worships the devil'.

Tradition has it that the people that lived in this compound were scattered at a point in the past due to some problems described as 'wars' but I never actually got to know the full story. We were told that the family homes got burnt down and every mother took her children to somewhere safe. My father did not return to this compound to live until the later part of his life, although he had always stated his intention to go back. He initially took his mother's home as his main home, and it was to be where he built a house which was our family home for many years.

My grandfather somehow became a Muslim but again I have not heard the story about how that happened. Neither have I heard any story about how he relocated from his town of birth to the town in the suburb of the city where he eventually settled and died. I know next to nothing about my grandfather apart from the fact that he established the first Islamic and Arabic School in that town. I reckon my grandfather's faith in Islam must have been strong because the people in the town where he settled at that time were known as an idol and masquerade worshipers.

What is described above is the context in which my father came to the world. His father had run away from an evil war in the town where he was born, along the way he apparently found some strong faith in Islam that eventually was to take him on a missionary journey. In this new community (which was also idol-worshipping), he became the chief Imam as he was the only Muslim and he started to teach the local people about Islam. The weight of expectation on my father was to live as a good Muslim and continue the missionary work of his father.

Islam Takes Its Grip

Although my father lived most of his formative years in communities steeped in idol worship he also had the benefit of 'Godly' faith upbringing through his father. I have not heard of any explanation for the decision to send my father to live with his uncle in his late teens but I can imagine that was because where his uncle lived was known for its large Muslim population and Islamic scholars.

My grandfather most likely sent his son to a place where he could learn and grow in his Islamic faith or to attempt correcting some emergent rebellious behaviour seen in his son. It is therefore not surprising to have found out recently that my father lived a more open faith life in this Islamic town before he became the 'perfect Muslim' his father wanted. I remember my father telling me that he used to drink alcohol and smoke cigarettes, behaviours that sadly many of his children also inherited. All of us inherited his strong-minded, stubborn, and often rebellious characteristics.

It took a while for the 'desired' type of Islam to get into my father but the traits started to be more noticeable around the time of my birth. I know this for certain because my father told me the story that he named me Kamal-deen as it means someone who is 'complete in Islam'. He also named me Adesina which means 'he opens the way' because he believed my birth paved the way for him to become more religious. My father wanted me to know the significance of my name and his hopes for me to be a good Muslim, an expectation that for many years became a stumbling block for me to accept Jesus into my life.

In any case, my father's religious faith in Islam was to enable him to clean up part of his life. He found the strength to stop smoking and drinking and became a 'good' person. The impact of the type of Islam in the town he lived in also started to show in his style of dressing such as wearing a turban and trousers which stopped above the ankles. He wore his beard long and insisted on his children going to Quranic Schools. He commanded his wives to stop working and live in seclusion as was the 'requirement' for Muslim women. So my father's change of lifestyle had a significant impact on his family.

Even though my father was brought up as a Muslim and had left the two idol-worshipping cultures where he was raised, he went back to his town of origin to marry his two main wives. Not surprisingly both of them also came from idol-worshipping families. My mother was from a royal family but they were well known for worshipping the town's river goddess. My mother, the only child of her mother, was said to have been a gift from the river goddess. My step-mother, judging from her compound name was also married from another idol-worshipping compound. The way these two women responded to my father's lifestyle change had a significant lasting effect on them and their children.

My older half-brother and I were the first children whom my father decided must go to Islamic School instead of mainstream schools. This was around when both of us were just completing our primary school education. I am forever grateful to my mother for standing her ground that I must go to mainstream secondary school as I know she must have fought very hard.

I don't think my mother won the argument with my father to allow me to go to school. I believe she just took the matter into her own hands and made the decision without my father's consent. That kind of action is no ordinary feat for an illiterate Muslim wife in those days and she would likely have suffered for it. She made the arrangements and sent me to live and school in a different town with our eldest sister who was married to a university lecturer and was living within the campus.

My mother's intervention and my eldest sister's support changed my life by allowing me to be educated and live within a learned community. My half-brother also escaped from going to the Quranic School because of my mother's intervention as my father's aim was to get a child from each wife to go for Islamic education. Unfortunately, my immediate younger brother and other half-brother did not have the same privilege as us and ended up having to go to the Quranic School.

Knowing my mother's love for her children and her hope for them to be properly educated, my younger brother going to Islamic school must have hurt her deeply. My mother never actually explained to me why she values education so much but I guess that it is because of her own experience. As the only female child of her mother in a royal family, she was not allowed to go to school as her half-brothers did and that must hurt. She was very determined to fight for her children's education. She must have been under tremendous pressure from everyone around her to be submissive to her husband's demands and she must have been labelled as a bad wife. At this same time, she was battling to keep her job and her independence as my father wanted both wives to stop working. She managed to keep her job but lost the battle to keep my younger brother out of the Quranic School.

One of my traumatic memories as a child during this period was eavesdropping on one of my father's Islamic friends and an uncle, at the back of our family vehicle. They were making derogatory comments about my mother because she was refusing to obey my father on these issues.

By reflecting on what my father was thinking at this time, I can now understand that he was consumed by his passion for Islam and was thinking ahead in terms of succession as to who was going to be the next Islamic scholar in the family. My younger brother was fortunate enough to be sent to a modern Islamic school and learned a lot of things to make him a 'good' religious person. My half-brother, on the other hand, was sent to learn from an Islamic Mullah where he picked up some bad religious practices. My younger brother, due to further intervention from my mum and second sister, was later sent to study Islamic education in a more recognised and balanced educational institution, in the town where my second sister got married. He was there for a couple of years before his premature death at 19.

A Bad Decision Or God's Calling?

Going back to my father; he was putting his house in order by sorting out himself, his wives, and his children in preparation for going full time as an Islamic scholar. Soon after, he decided to sell off his successful contractor partnership business and return to the town in the city suburb to carry on the work of his father as Imam of the first Quranic and Arabic School. As part of his generous nature and zeal for the Islamic faith, he did not intend to run the Islamic School for business as he believed in providing free Islamic education to the people. He intended to use the proceeds from the sale of his partnership company to establish another business in the city that would provide income for his needs as an Islamic scholar. I remember he was particularly interested in exploring the saw-mill business.

My father did not start a saw-mill business or any business for that matter. His plan for self-sufficiency, therefore, did not work out and all the money he went to the city with eventually went down the drain. I supposed I was too young at that time to understand what happened but I guess that the many dependants he had to cater for and his over-generosity meant that the money was gone before he realised what was happening.

My recollection of the period between when my father sold his business and when all the money was gone was of having a good and happy life. We had a lot of money and we carried plenty of cash around in those days. I think it was around the time when the currency was being changed over in our country. I remember us as children stealing a few notes from among the bundles of money we carried around from bank to bank, where my father was trying to change the notes. I have of course repented and asked God to forgive me for this sin and I hope my siblings have done the same.

Once again, my mother's independent streak and determination was a well needed positive intervention for our family. Whilst my step-mother eagerly went ahead with my father on his full-time Islamic scholar adventure, my mother refused to move to the city but instead chose to remain where she was in her civil service job as a cook in a secondary boarding school. This decision meant she was able to continue providing for her children regardless of my father's financial situation. She eventually worked until her full retirement age and is now benefiting from her pensions. My mother never lived in the city with my father and she only returned to live with him after he returned to his parents' town of origin.

My father's loss of fortune and lack of personal income did not have an apparent or direct negative impact on him, however, because fortunately for him, his first daughter had finished university and was married to a lecturer from a well-to-do family. His next two children also finished university and subsequently relocated to the United States of America. Together, the first three children were able to cater for our father's needs.

But the situation is more complex because my father's needs also included taking care of his second wife and all her children, running the not-for-profit Islamic School as well as catering for the needs of an innumerable number of extended family, which was not sustainable. This remains a major problem in the family as the dependant culture of relatives has become expected and seems beyond any hope of change.

Apparently, the tendency for excessive generosity is part of the fabric of the country's culture. A recent United Nations population statistics report shows that an average working adult in the country supports four other people outside of their immediate family. This, on one hand, is something to be celebrated as it shows the kindness of people to one another but it does also lead to a dependency culture if not properly managed.

Apart from the financial burden, or perhaps, as a result, my father's ability to live in the city became harder and harder after being faced with one problem after the other. One of my younger half-brothers lost his hearing after apparently been beaten with a magic whip from a masquerade. My younger brother died in mysterious circumstances; my step-mother also died after a mysterious brief illness. People in the area outside of the family also started causing problems and laying claim to the land given to my grandfather and we had to settle by more or less buying back the land.

Relatives and friends who were also dependent on what he received from his children surrounded my father. These people would get the money from him in any way they could, but they didn't need to work hard as my father gave generously.

To cap it all, my father's health started to decline rapidly and all these things led to a discussion about his final return to his parents' town of origin. As already requested by my father, a house was built for him on the site of his original family home. He decided or was encouraged to finally return to his parents' town of origin to live out the rest of his life. My mother, who was by then retired from her job and was living in the town where my father left her, was also persuaded to return to look after her now frail husband. She did this devotedly until he passed away.

Perhaps the most positive outcome of my father's move to the city was the fact that he managed to reclaim the land that was originally given to his father (which is now occupied by my half-siblings). Another outcome was my father's ability to reinstate the Islamic and Arabic school started by his father, at least for a while until his physical and financial ability to maintain the school dwindled to the extent that it became impossible. Seeing the Arabic school fail must have been quite difficult for him and he tried his best to get others to keep it going but that became an impossible task without a child in the family willing to take the scholarly or financial responsibility.

Up till his return to his father's town of origin, my father learned, married, worked, raised a family, and went to do his part in moving on the spiritual work of his father. He must have felt satisfied that he found and accepted the Islamic faith along the journey and he worked hard to be the best Muslim he could.

My father subsequently returned home to enjoy the rest of his life, to die in peace, and then hopefully spend eternity in Al-Jannah which is known in Islam as Paradise. Unfortunately, a Muslim never knows if he has done enough to earn the favour of Allah and paradise unless of course, he goes to his death by martyrdom – an ideology that has been used by some to recruit terrorists looking for a back door to paradise. There was, therefore, no way that my father could have fully known that he was going to paradise as a Muslim. In the next chapter, I will describe how I believe my father had found the only certain way to paradise.

Is Faith Exchange Possible?

Perhaps my most common and fervent prayer since my conversion to Christianity has been the salvation of my relatives and most especially my father. I naturally put my father's salvation first as he was the oldest, most poorly in health and also the head of the clan. I was aware that many of his relatives blindly followed his faith in Islam which made me believe that was he to convert it could change the course of my extended family's faith history.

My journey of faith in interceding and praying for my extended family's salvation has been complex, daunting, exhausting, invigorating, and filled with several ups and downs. I have experienced moments of exceeding joy and encouragement when I caught glimpses of what God was doing in some of my relative's lives. But I have also experienced many moments of sadness, frustration, and fear for the souls of my relatives should they die or should Jesus return before their salvation.

However, through all these experiences, I can boldly testify of God's love, faithfulness, grace and

His desire for everyone including all my relatives to come to the knowledge of our Lord Jesus and receive the gift of salvation. I believe and I have received a few prophetic declarations that part of the reason God saved me is so that I can intercede for the rest of my family. I remember someone said to me after praying that I am like the Joseph of my family and God had sent me ahead to save my relatives. I am even now more convinced that my heavenly Father has called every one of my relatives because He answers my prayers. He will send Jesus to all of them and thereby allow them to decide to follow Him to eternal life.

From what I have read and seen around the world about Muslims who have converted to Christianity and using myself as a case study, I can say I have some understanding of how difficult it is for someone from a strong Islamic background to accept Jesus Christ as their Lord and Saviour. My impression and experience are that Muslims can be in a kind of spiritual bondage that requires a supernatural encounter with Jesus through dreams, visions, miraculous interventions, or healing before they can be born again. This is partly because the Islamic religion is steeped in dogmatic followership and people are not encouraged to question their faith or the authenticity of the Quran.

Many Islamic scholars have used a quote in the Quran which says 'do not ask about things which, if they are shown to you, will distress you' to impress on Muslims not to question their faith in Islam. They usually leave out the fact the same passage also states that 'if you ask about them while the Qur'an is being revealed, they will be shown to you' (Quran 5:101). Unfortunately, many people take what their religious leaders have told them rather than studying the scriptures themselves and asking God to reveal the truth to them.

Another major factor that could prevent freedom from Islam is the physical danger, intimidation, and relationship trauma that is likely to arise as a result of a Muslim's conversion to Christianity. The intimidation I experienced and the trauma of the hurt and shame I thought I was going to cause my relatives, especially my parents, was part of the reason I ignored the Lord's calling on my life for very many years. I also know personally of at least two close relatives who are in the same situation I was right now. My prayer is that my story will inspire them to know they can also choose to be free and live openly as Christ's Disciples.

I thank God for the amazing testimony I have and the many examples of people who have managed to break out of Islam and other religions they have not chosen to follow. The determination to face and then escape the threat of persecution or even death and the obvious transformation for good in the lives of such converted people will surely continue to be an inspiration to those who are still in bondage.

My father, in his clever humorous way, would always find a way to talk about my new faith. He initially tried to discourage me by reminding me of his journey and the meaning of my name. He later debated and discussed the similarities and differences between Islam and Christianity and later on, he acknowledged the power of healing that is available through Jesus. My father in the last few months of his life would switch to English when talking about my faith or asking about the Church so that his wife (my mum) would not understand what we were talking about as she does not speak English.

The period when I was able to have face to face discussions of faith with my father was during my family's two-week visit to the country a year and a half before his death. This was our first time of meeting after he knew I was a Christian as I had not been home for the previous ten years. He did not show any anger or disappointment about my change of religion. Instead, he was quite receptive and listened to my explanation of what had made me accept Jesus Christ into my life. He was appreciative of the gift of money that was sent to him by the Pastor from our Church.

He invited my wife and me to pray for his sight to get better as he had lost it a few months before. I remembered we laid hands on my father as we prayed for his sight to be restored. He called us back to pray some more as his sight got better after the first prayer. I remember telling him the story of the blind man Jesus healed of his sight who initially saw men like trees before Jesus prayed for him again to receive his full sight (Mark 8:22-26).

As I prayed for my father the second time, I remember praying that the eyes of his heart may be opened to know Christ as I recognised that his salvation miracle was more important than him regaining his physical sight. I knew my father was going to die at some point and his physical sight was not as important as having eternal life with Christ. At this point, I recognised that I had the battle to fight for my father's soul.

I am very grateful to God that my father was open enough to have a conversation and even debate with me about my faith in Jesus Christ. This type of openness was encouraging as it was not found in many of my other relatives.

Battle For A Loved Father's Soul

One of my main prayers over the last few years has been that my father would not die before he gave his life to Jesus. I believe God answered this prayer and part of the answer was granting my father many extensions to his life on earth.

There were several occasions in the last few years when people thought my father was going to die but he always seemed to miraculously recover. I heard stories of many of his friends visiting him whilst sick and saying their final goodbyes to him only for them to end up dying before he did. He eventually outlived most of his closest friends. On a few occasions relatives have also paid visits thinking it would be the last, but my father always bounced back to life. My siblings made sure we threw a big birthday party for him two years ago as an opportunity to capture his life story and take pictures with the family but the Lord extended his life for another two years.

His many recoveries from 'old age illnesses' meant that people started to suspect that there was black magic preventing my him from dying, insinuating that he must have 'eaten' something to prevent it. My older sister was approached during my father's last illness that she should make a certain sacrifice to undo whatever my father had done to prevent his death which she vehemently declined.

But that does not mean other 'concerned' relatives did not try to help my father die. I think there is an unspoken rule in the local context that an older person who is no longer independent but relying on others for his day to day living is better off dead than alive. I suppose this is due to the concern about financial, physical, and emotional burden of care on others, as well as the concern for the apparent pain or loss of dignity of the older person. In the last two days of my father's life, I observed a suspicious exchange between an Islamic Mullah and a close relative and a subsequent action from the close relative that made me suspect they tried something. I have no proof of this happening and it was just a split second spiritual insight. But what is more important is that I know no one could have speeded up my father's death unless God allowed that to happen for His good purpose.

Anyway, as I continued in my prayers of intercession for my father's soul to be saved, I was also looking for opportunities to minister directly to him when we spoke on the phone. I thought about ways I could get to him through other people who have become Christians within the extended family. The first relative I thought could minister to my father was a second cousin who was very open and strong about his faith as a Christian and has become a Pastor.

He had always prayed for my father and would also share the gospel with him when he visited. This cousin told me that on one occasion when my father was sick and unable to get up, he prayed for him in the name of Jesus to 'take up his mat and walk' and my father was then able to walk. I believe this was true but that apparent miracle did not convert my father to a Christian. I was, however, unable to rely on this cousin to minister to my father much as I was not always in contact with him and also because the way he portrayed Christianity to the family was not well received. To my relatives, he was hostile and offensive in the way he talked or challenged other people's faith. His poor and unkempt appearance did not earn him much respect in the family either. To me, he is a kind of role model as he is willing to proclaim the Lordship of Jesus irrespective of the personal cost to himself.

Then there was my aunt, my father's youngest half-sister, who became a Christian as a result of marrying one. This aunt was very close to my father; she lived in the same town and visited him almost every day when he was ill. I had several telephone discussions with her about my father. I encouraged her to talk to him about Jesus and lead him in a prayer to accept Jesus as his personal Lord and Saviour whenever she felt my father was ready.

My aunt's view, however, was that leading my father in a prayer of repentance would not be necessary because he was a good man and so he would find his way to heaven. She explained that it does not matter whether someone is a Muslim or Christian and that as long they are good people they will make it to heaven. This is possibly a common belief in families where you have people of both faiths as I heard the same from another two people in the family during my last trip.

I suppose that having this sort of belief is a coping mechanism so as not to have the conflict between relatives who have different religious faiths. This syncretic belief that every faith leads to heaven is now rampant all over the world. But the Bible describes this belief system as the broad way that leads to destruction (Matthew 7:13).

I was of course very disappointed about my aunt's response as I firmly believe in Jesus' statement in John 14:6 that 'I am the way and the truth and the life. No one comes to the Father except through me'. I can understand why my aunt believed my father was good; after all, as we found out in a recent document, it was my father who donated one of his properties (a shop) to her, thirteen years ago. This is another example of my father's generosity but this aunt was good to us also when she had money and I don't think any of us would begrudge her having the property. I must, however, have further discussions with my aunt to try and correct her erroneous belief that every one good makes it to heaven.

You may want to ask at this stage; what about me, could I not lead my father in a prayer of salvation? This was a question I also asked myself some times. I was in my ninth year of following Jesus and I have experienced tremendous growth in my faith. I have had a few experiences of leading individuals in the sinner's prayer to accept Jesus as their Lord and Saviour. I am comfortable sharing my faith and the gospel in all sorts of scenarios and I am a part of a door-knocking ministry in my Church. So why did I not attempt to lead my father in the prayer to accept Jesus Christ into his life?

The simple answer I can honestly give is that I did not believe my father was ready. Our conversations since I had last seen him had been only for a few minutes, mostly every week when I phoned home. By then my father did not have a phone so I would call my mother who would take the phone to him for us to have a conversation. These were usually quite short because my mother would be waiting with him for us to finish so that she could take the phone back. Sometimes my father would be weak and not able to say more than a few words of greeting or the phone connection would be so bad that I could hardly hear him.

Despite these constraints, we still managed to have a few interesting discussions. He would usually ask about the Church and the Pastor, if everyone was okay and if I was still going to Church. I would often pray for him or tell him Jesus loves him during these conversations but I never really felt it was appropriate to ask him if he wanted to pray to accept Jesus into his life. Perhaps also subconsciously I had already realised that it would take a supernatural encounter for my father to be born again[2].

In the last few months of his life, a member of my 'Church in the Home'[3] suggested that we should be praying for such a supernatural encounter as she also strongly believed that it would take this to convert a Muslim. From then this started to be added into my prayers. Such an encounter with Jesus also became part of my conversation with my father even though I was not aware of what and how that was going to happen.

My last exchange of words with him took place on 26th February, exactly a month before he died. I had not had a chance to call on the previous Sunday which is my usual 'phone home day' and calling from the office meant I did not have much time. He was quite chatty on this occasion which was unusual at that time as he hadn't been feeling well.

He almost immediately went into English-speaking mode and asked me about the Church. 'How are your church and your Pastor?' he asked. To be honest I do not remember most of the conversation as I did not want to engage given I was busy in the office. I do remember clearly saying to him, 'Jesus is going to come to you in a dream, please listen to him and say 'yes' when he asks you to give your life to him.' I do not remember my father's response but in all honesty, neither was I listening for one. The phone was soon passed back to my mother and that was the end of the conversation. The conversation with my father was later that evening shared as a testimony and prayer request in my Church in The Home.

The following Sunday I received a phone call from my elder brother from the United States who told me that when he phoned home that day he was told our father was found ill in the morning and unable to speak. He did not speak again until he died about a month later. But as described earlier, my father becoming unwell was not unusual at that stage of his life. The loss of speech was a first, but still, I don't think anybody was hugely concerned and we all expected him to bounce back to life as usual.

My brother had arranged a private doctor for my father and the initial report was that he was very dehydrated and the main treatment was to restore his fluid balance. This carried on for about a week with no noticeable improvement and my father was still unable to speak. As usual, my siblings in the country and other relatives started to visit him just in case it was going to be their last goodbye.

Surprisingly my elder brother in the US told me he had also decided to go and see our father. His decision to travel perhaps gave me the first indication that the illness was quite serious this time as my brother was the person liaising directly with the doctor and was more informed of the prognosis. When he arrived he initiated more medical investigations including blood tests and an MRI. My father was also admitted to a private hospital for a couple of days whilst waiting for the results of these tests.

My main action at the time all this was going on was to go deeper into prayer and fasting for intercession. My main prayer points were salvation and healing for my father, salvation being the top priority. My specific prayer was that Jesus Christ would meet with my father as I unknowingly prophesied to him and that my father would be open to receive the gift of salvation. The same prayer requests were shared in my Church in the Home, the main Church, our church night vigil[4], our Christian fellowship at work, and other friends that I prayed with. The first answers to our prayers were the way God ministered and prepared me for the journey ahead.

Spiritual Preparation For Battle

As I continued in prayer and fasting for my father's salvation I had a short dream which I believe was relevant to the situation. But before I describe this dream I need to tell you that I rarely dream, or at least I don't usually remember my dreams. You may find that unbelievable for someone like me who came to faith in Christ based on a recurring dream of his second coming. But actually, those fifteen years of receiving the saving visions were the highlights of my dreaming experience. I have a very small dream book I have kept for the last six years and only twelve dreams have been recorded so far.

In my dream, I was lying in bed asleep. I opened my eyes to see the shape of a man standing beside the bed. I could see it was a man's body, probably a young man's body as it looked fit judging by the tone of the muscles. From the neck up was empty with a covering like a black sack where the head was supposed to be. What I immediately realised in the dream was that I was not afraid of the man whereas I should have naturally been afraid of a headless figure standing almost on top of me while I slept. Instead, the man by the way he positioned

33

his arms appeared to me like someone asking for my help.

In my dream, I started praying in the name of Jesus for Satan to come out of the body. I remember praying that 'I take authority in the name of Jesus for you Satan to get out of this body'. I then heard some groaning noise in my ear that sounds like 'out' and 'ouch' as if the demon was in pain. I then woke up.

I did not immediately connect this dream to my father until I started to narrate it to my wife in the morning. It was only then that I realised the body could have been my father's and that I was interceding for him in the spirit. His actual physical body was old, frail, and passing away but his spiritual body was young and fit. I was very grateful for the revelation in the dream and I thanked God for the power available to me in the name of Jesus. From then on I believed the battle was won and I started to thank God for answering my prayers and the gift of salvation and deliverance for my father.

Another significant spiritual help for me at the time was that my Pastor had long before given me a topic to preach on in our church entitled 'Strengthened in the Inner Being' and this was to be delivered the Sunday after the dream and before I had to travel to see my father. The teaching was part of the Church's series of teaching on Authentic Christianity – God's covenant people. The sermon was based on Apostle Paul's prayers for the Ephesian Church (Ephesians 3:14-21).

I believe that God used my preparation for this particular sermon to equip and strengthen me for what was going to happen with regards to my father. It turned out that I was fully prepared and ready for everything that happened during his final sickness, the final battle for his soul, his death, and the arrangements for his burial that followed. By this time I had realised that it was time for him to die. I believed that God would answer my prayers for my father but what I needed was strength to keep interceding for him up till the last seconds of his life. I shared during the sermon that I needed inner strength to overcome the fear that people I dearly love may miss out on the gift of salvation.

As earlier described, my older brother had started taking our father through further medical tests and as the results came in we could all see the extent of his illness. He was eventually diagnosed with advanced prostate cancer which had spread to his spinal cord and his brain also leading to brain haemorrhage. We were advised that due to the extent of the cancer spread and his age, there was no viable medical option to save his life. My father was discharged home after a couple of days in the hospital and the advice was to continue with palliative care at home. I did have an opportunity to pray directly for him when he was admitted to the hospital. My half-brother was the one who stayed with our father overnight in the hospital and he kindly allowed me to pray for him even though I told him specifically I was going to pray for our father in Jesus's name.

My half-brother confirmed that my father's sense of hearing was still intact so I asked him to put his phone to my father's ear so I could use the opportunity to share the gospel and pray with him. I used that opportunity again to reassure my father that Jesus loved him, that he would surely meet with him if he had not done so already and I invited my father to commit his life to Jesus. He was by then unable to talk so I could not get a response from him.

My father's doctor gave an end of life prognosis of three to six months. I then felt that I could still make it to him before he died. He, however, did not last more than a week after the diagnosis of his illness.

One aspect of my father's illness that amazed me and I am grateful for was the apparent lack of pain despite the extensive spread of cancerous cells in his body. My father did not show any evidence of pain or discomfort until he took his last breath. He had a bit of temperature now and again and showed some involuntary jerky movements but otherwise, he was settled and resting for the last few days of his life.

I am also grateful for my father's sense of hearing remaining seemingly intact until he took his last breath. I have heard people say that hearing is always the last to go before someone dies. I was certain this was what happened with my father because up to the last minutes of his life he was still responding to requests for him to open his mouth and to swallow his food and medicine.

My decision to travel to see my father was made very quickly. My elder brother after spending a week with him informed me that he needed to return to the US. My older sister also based in the US wanted to go but she was having some problems in renewing her passport. I therefore quickly made up my mind to go and replace my brother and also help carry some of the financial burdens of our father's on-going treatment. I bought a ticket and arranged to travel for two weeks so I could spend some time with my father. It turned out that my sister decided to travel anyway on her expiring passport. It was good in the end that I did not know of my sister's decision before I bought my ticket as I would have probably thought it would make more sense to let her go first and for me to go when she had left.

My sister and I arrived in the country on the same day. The same car and relatives that took my older brother to the airport for his return flight to the United States of America waited to take me and my sister home.

Before I narrate the final battle of the last two days, I want to share another spiritual experience I had when praying for my father before I undertook the journey to see him. I believe God gave me three Bible passages, and these I read every day for about a week before I travelled, and every day when I was in the country.

The three passages were Psalm 23, Psalm 91, and 1 Kings 18:16-40. My understanding when I received the scriptures was that the two psalms were for my protection and I believe that was quite obvious. I understood 1 Kings 18 which describes the confrontation between the Prophet Elijah and the combined 850 prophets of Baal and Asherah[5] was a prophetic declaration of the battle for my father's soul. This will hopefully be clearer as I describe the last couple of days of my father's life. I believe these passages were from God but I must say that I am still learning to discern the different ways God speaks with me. Nevertheless, I try to take it seriously any time I believe I have heard directly from God.

Taking A Position For Battle – Can I Be Like Elijah?

As I write about the last two days of my father's life and my involvement in his journey, I need to pause to reflect on the significance of the 1 Kings 18: 16-40 passage which I believe God gave me for reassurance that the battle is His and is already won.

As I was putting this in writing I also remembered that God gave me the exact three Bible passages when we visited the country as a family about a year and a half before my father died. Does this mean these passages are to be a permanent revelation each time I go there? Only time will tell. Also as I cast my mind back to the previous journey, I cannot say I saw a big manifestation or application of that prophetic passage. But I remember at least a couple of incidents that brought the passage to my mind.

During that trip, we went to visit my eldest sister and her husband in their home. Before that visit, I had not had any conversation with this sister about my faith but I was aware that both she and her husband knew about it. Our visit happened to take place on a Friday afternoon and my sister proposed that she will go to the mosque first for the Friday Jumat service and after that, we would go out together. So we drove after them to the mosque and parked outside whilst my sister and her husband went in to pray. After they finished praying and we were ready to move on, my sister's car would not start. Her husband tried several times but the ignition did not start. He opened the car bonnet and knocked a few things around but the car still did not start.

I offered to try and help start the car and as I took the key I remembered the contest between Elijah and the 850 prophets of Baal and Asherah. My heart was pounding fast within my chest as I prayed quietly within me for the God that answered Elijah by fire to fire up the car's engine. Sure enough, the car started after my first or second attempt to turn the key! Hurrah!! I was overwhelmed with joy and almost expected my sister to catch my faith in Christ based on that victory!

But there was no chance of anyone joining me in praising God as I did not tell anyone about what He was going to do! Nevertheless, my faith soared higher based on that experience as I believe the same God who answered Prophet Elijah by fire to ignite a sacrifice doused with plenty of water is the same God who answered my prayer to fire up an internal combustion engine with a starter that didn't work!

The second time I remembered the Elijah battle was when I had a telephone showdown with the same sister just before I left the country. She had phoned me to have a conversation about what made me become a Christian. She said she could not bear to talk to me face to face but she just had to bare her heart to me before I left. This was strange because my sister did not acknowledge my new faith when we saw her even though her husband remarked on it a few times.

Anyway, I was actually on my knees praying when my sister called and we had about half an hour conversation. I was able to tell her about my experience of Christ in the visions and how my life has been transformed since then. My sister tried to pose contrary arguments to everything I said and insinuated that I was brainwashed, tricked, drugged, and so on.

But what my sister could not deny was the transforming power of Christ in my life and she is the one person that knew me when I was really bad (more of that in part two). I believe she must have seen the changed person I had become even with the short time we spent together. I did apologise to her for the troubles I had caused her as a teenager living under her care and I hope she was able to forgive me. We finished the telephone

conversation with a wager from my sister that we
would talk again after six months when I would be
back to my senses. I am still waiting for that next
conversation to happen!

I have a feeling the above couple of stories may
be a bit disappointing for you and not what you
will expect as a strong show of faith when you put
it side by side with the confrontation between
Elijah and the Prophets of Baal and Asherah!
However, I wholeheartedly believe that my God is
the same yesterday, today, and forevermore
(Hebrews 13:8). He can replicate the miracles of
old in bigger or smaller measure depending on the
faith of his disciple and ultimately according to his
purpose for that generation. I know that the more
I step out in faith, the more miracles I will see in
my lifetime.

I know definitely that I am no Elijah, not now
anyway! But I know that I am still a work in
progress so who knows what may happen in the
future. In any case, I did not read too much into
the 1 Kings 18 passage that I was given two years
ago neither did I read too much into it two years
later as I prepared to go home for the final battle
for my father's soul. However, I was diligent and
faithful enough to read and pray daily using the
three passages I believe I was given for the trips.

The 1 Kings 18 passage was helpful to remind
me that I was in a spiritual battle in which I was

the minority in terms of numbers. It was me and few other people who were praying against the majority of my extended family who knew my father was a Muslim Imam, an Islamic scholar, and who they believed wanted to die as a Muslim. Ordinarily, I might have felt I stood no chance but my faith was big enough to believe nothing is impossible for my God.

I have had opportunities to reflect in recent times on my relationship with my extended Muslim family and the role I can take to witness to them. I did not and I still do not believe the Lord has called me to take a strong position like that of Prophet Elijah and challenge my Muslim relatives to an open contest. The position I believe God wanted me to take at that moment was mainly that of spiritual warfare in prayer and intercession for the lives of every soul in my extended family. The next strategy was to be a representative of Jesus to my family in the way I relate to them and thirdly to share the gospel of Christ or my testimony of salvation with them as best as I can when the opportunity presents itself. All these thoughts had already been settled in my mind as I arrived home to see my father.

The Final Battle

As we were driven home that night from the airport, I was quietly preparing myself for the battle. But at the same time, I was confident that I could overcome because I know that 'He who lives in me is greater than who is in the world' (1 John 4:4). I knew all I had to do was to be present on the battlefield and not give up at any time until the end and I believe God prepared me for that. I am grateful to God that the final face to face battle was finished within forty-eight hours for I don't think I would have had enough strength to carry on if it went on much further. My God already knew that so he prepared me accordingly.

When we arrived home there were many other people around who had come to see my father. We said a quick hello to my mother and then went to him. My sister went first to greet my father and cried over him. He was non-responsive as I hugged him and kissed him on the cheek. I told him that I loved him and that my wife and children also sent their love. Seeing the way he was I again realised that his time on earth was coming to an end.

Four other people were already preparing to sleep in my father's room: these were my uncle, my older half-brother, and two younger half-sisters. My older sister who arrived with me was going to sleep in the guest room. The uncle made way for me on the mattress so I could settle next to my father and my half-brother was on the other side of the mattress.

Meanwhile, before we were allowed to get to sleep, there was a congregation of Islamic prayers, initiated and led by my older sister from the US. I was always expected to sit through these prayer sessions which happened several times during the two days before my father died and carried on for another week after his death. These usually consisted of one or more people reading certain chapters of the Quran, especially the chapters the Muslims believe would help someone to make it to paradise. They usually tried to engage my father in the prayers and placed a 'rosary' in his hand so he could count along with the doctrinal statements.

All my siblings and most of our close relatives knew that I had become a Christian and that I do not pray as they do but I had no say in the type of prayers being said for my father. No one thought to ask at any time if I wanted to pray a Christian prayer for him. Ironically, I know that were my father able to voice out a prayer request, he would have asked for me to pray for him in Jesus's name. I know this from my last visit when he was open to being prayed for in Jesus's name. So that is exactly what I did; each time people were praying and reciting the Quran, I was praying in the Spirit[6]. Mostly I prayed in a quiet mode but sometimes audibly in the Spirit when my 'tongue' could not be differentiated from the Arabic language being used to recite the Quran.

Part of the reason I believe Islam can be a difficult religion to break from, especially in non-Arabic speaking countries such as in West Africa is because of illiteracy and indoctrination. The majority of my relatives praying through the Quran can only recite the words either because they can read Arabic letters or they have memorised the passage but most of them do not know the meaning of what they are reading. This majority relies on the Mullahs or the Islamic Scholars who explain to the people what they want them to understand.

One can argue that the same ignorance and dogmatic following of religious leaders exist in Christianity. It is also common to see Christian congregations where people blindly follow a Pastor or a so-called Prophet but in my experience, I don't think that is as common as in Islam. In any case, the Bible and authentic Christianity instruct believers to seek the truth for themselves whereas Islam apparently discourages interrogating the authenticity of the Quran or going against the interpretation of the Mullahs.

The First Night

As I laid down next to my father that first night, I did not have to think much about what to pray for. I did not pray a single prayer for him to be healed, I knew his time was up and my only prayer now was for the salvation of his soul. That first night was both physically and mentally exhausting for me considering I had just arrived from a long journey and I did not get any sleep. But there were a couple of significant events to narrate.

At a point late in the evening, I realised that all those visiting had left my father's room, leaving those of us who I thought was going to sleep there. Without much thought, I took out my phone and took some pictures of me and my father lying side by side on the mattress, a couple of the pictures were when he lifted my hand in the air with his. I then also made a video recording of me talking to my father about Jesus. In it, I was saying to my father, "Jesus Christ is Lord and He loves you. All you have to do is said yes to Him". I repeated this three times. I had to terminate the video recording abruptly when I heard my second half-sister coming back into the room to sleep.

To be honest I do not recollect my intention in taking the pictures and video described above. I only really thought about it after arriving back home and showing the pictures to my wife and she asked 'Is that how you want to remember your father?' I still can't answer that question with much conviction and all I can do now is reflect on my mindset then.

Were the recordings a selfish wish to assure myself that I was there and doing everything I could to save my father? Was I thinking I could capture a moment where he would open his mouth and audibly proclaim Jesus as Lord, so I could have evidence to share as a testimony to God's glory or God forbid, so I could boast about the victory? Was I reading too much into my mute father lifting my hand in the air as if he was agreeing with my statement that Jesus is Lord? All I can do now and have done is to repent of any bad motive on my part and ask God to forgive me of my sins whether deliberate or not. Thank God that 'the Blood of Jesus covers all unrighteousness and purifies us from all sins' (1 John 1:7).

In any case, once again unlike Elijah, but more like a thief caught in the act, I quickly shut down the video recording when I heard my half-sister walking into the room. Would the outcome in terms of evidence of my father's salvation have been more obvious if I had stood my ground, if I had more faith to say to my half-sister, 'Little sister - watch and see the power of my God as my father opens his mouth to confirm Jesus is Lord'?

Honestly, I don't think so. Not because my God cannot perform such miracles, but because I never heard God instructing me to take the pictures or record the video. All I have from this is a video and a few pictures as proof that I was there with my father, that he held my hand up in the air, and that I told him about Jesus. I don't think the recording is of any use to me or my father as we both certainly will remember that moment for eternity with or without photographic evidence.

I shall now narrate the second significant event that happened on the first night as those of us in the room settled down for the night. My father and I were on the same double mattress on the floor and I lay on his right-hand-side next to the wall. My half-brother was on the left and he slept right through the night. On the other end of the room at the foot of the mattress slept my uncle, my two half-sisters, and two young children of my older half-sister. My uncle, the older of the half-sisters and the two little children more or less slept through the night.

I started praying more confident and audible prayers once I realised everybody was asleep. I felt that now I could pray aloud in the Spirit without disturbing or causing offence to anyone. I would go into silent prayer mode and pretend I was asleep whenever I saw anyone moving or seemingly about to wake up. Imagine my shock and frustration when at some point during the night my younger half-sister woke up and sat up facing my father and me and started reading something from an open book on her lap!

Apart from this preventing me from being able to pray audibly, I was seriously concerned about what she was doing, as I thought she must be engaged in a cultic activity involving some kind of incantation. These thoughts flashed through my mind as I remembered she was the half-sister who went to learn a trade in traditional nursing which means the use of herbs and black magic to treat an illness.

My response was to go into another round of silent spiritual warfare in prayer. I was not afraid of this kind of engagement and I was confident that no matter what she was up to, her power could in no way withstand the name of Jesus. So there I was pretending to be asleep but praying in the Spirit to counter whatever evil incantation was coming from my half-sister and still praying in the Spirit for my father's salvation. I almost shouted out in victory after what seemed like several hours but was probably only half an hour when she finished what she was doing and went back to sleep.

So that was how the first night went: I started badly by taking an unplanned, unauthorised and possibly wrongly motivated photo and video recording, I did what I could in staying awake and praying mostly in quietness and in the spirit for my father and then I went through a supposed spiritual battle with my half-sister.

Firstly I have to thank God for the provision of His Holy Spirit which enables us, His children, to pray all kinds of prayers, and to pray in tongues which are then interpreted by the Holy Spirit according to the will of God.

Thank God, the encounter with my half-sister during the night became an unexpected testimony in the morning when I finally realised what had happened. I was pleasantly surprised when I summoned some courage to ask her why she was up to during the night and what she was doing. I was full of joy when she told me that she had secretly become a Christian and now attends a church. She then proceeded to show me the prayer book from her church which she was praying from during the night. She explained to me that the teaching from her church is 'whenever you wake up in the night, pick up the prayer book and pray'. We were both praying on the same side!

Whoah! What an amazing God I serve. I thought I was fighting an enemy during the night but actually, Jesus already gained victory and provided me a sister within the family. I realised that this was no longer a half-sister to me but a full sister in the Lord, praise God! That early morning revelation was an encouragement for me on what was to be the last day of my father's life.

The Day Before The Last

What happened in my home when I was a child was that by 5.30 am everybody was woken to go to the mosque for morning prayers. As I write this I remember the method used by a particular uncle who lived with us in contrast to that used by my mother, but more of that is in part two of this book.

So at 5.30 am in my father's sickroom on that last day, everybody woke up or was awoken to go and pray in the mosque. Thankfully I was not part of the group. Everyone quickly left to go to the mosque leaving me, my father, and my new sister in the Lord behind.

That was when she was able to share her testimony with me that she is now a Christian. She was still not bold enough to tell others in the family about her new faith so I encouraged her to be strong and that she would be alright. I resolved to keep in contact with her to give continued encouragement.

The fact that almost everybody was away for the morning prayers gave me a further opportunity to talk to my father, to share the gospel with him, pray for him and tell him how much I loved him. These were the really special times I had with my father when it was just the two of us and my Christian half-sister and I could say anything I wanted. I heard myself repeating a lot of times that Jesus loved him and that Jesus is the only one who could give him eternal life. I also continued to pray a lot in the Spirit whilst hopefully looking for signs that my father had accepted the gift of salvation through Jesus Christ.

The rest of the day, despite all other things that happened, was uneventful as far as I was concerned. We washed my father in bed, changed his clothes and bedding, and then gave him breakfast of a few spoonfuls of pap. He took his pain relief tablet prescribed by his doctor and was laid back down in bed. This was immediately followed by another round of Islamic prayer and reading of the Quran led by my older sister. As usual, I sat through the sessions but praying quietly in the Spirit.

My father's doctor arrived at about 9 am for his daily morning visit; he checked my father's vitals and administered two injections. To us children, these appeared very painful but the doctor assured us that it is better he has the injections to prevent pain.

My older sister from the US and I then met with the doctor privately and he explained to us the results of investigations carried out, the treatment options, and his view that palliative care was the only reasonable option. My sister has more medical knowledge, as she is a pharmacist, and so asked most of the questions and discussed the options. I and my sister discussed this after the doctor had left and agreed that he was just being kind by his hopeful prognosis in order not to cause us much distress. After that, other people started coming to visit my father and that carried on throughout the day.

My father's younger half-brother, my uncle, who is the next head of the family after my father, was one of them. This uncle, who we all call 'our small father', was very involved and helpful in everything that concerned my parents and our family home. He was instrumental in my father returning home from the city, building the family home, encouraging my mother to return home, and being the person that helped sort out all sorts of practical issues as they arose. My relatives all have a wide range of opinions about this uncle and so do I.

But what can be easily described was that this uncle stood by us and supported us in everything we did. He visited us most days before my father died and also afterward even though his wife was seriously ill and was going in and out of the hospital for treatment. She is also a Christian and

I am glad that I managed to visit her and pray for her and encouraged her before I left.

Other relatives arrived through the day to come and see my father. My eldest sister and her husband, my youngest sister and her husband, other relatives, the Mullahs from surrounding mosques, and friends of the family also came to visit. Most visitors would come to my father's room and spend a few minutes talking to him or about him. Some, especially the Mullahs would choose to pray, mostly in the Islamic way such as by reading parts of the Quran.

I sat through most of the day in my father's room welcoming the visitors, listening to their stories, jokes, prayers, etc. I don't remember much of the conversation or the people who visited and I did not enjoy what I considered to be an intrusion on our private family time. But I understand that my father was a very popular and much-loved person and that it would be impossible or rude to prevent people from seeing him. The doctor returned for another visit in the afternoon and carried out a repeat of the morning's test. He reported that there was no change of note.

As it was a Sunday, some people who had travelled to visit were also returning home to resume work on Monday. My eldest and youngest sisters and their spouses returned to their bases. My youngest half-sister who was now my sister-in-Christ also left, and by the evening the older half-sister who lives in the town also returned home.

The Last Night

So when night came, it was only my father and me, my half-brother and my younger uncle left in the room. As we got ready to sleep and were talking, I found out some encouraging information about the two men. I discovered that my half-brother who I knew was separated from his wife had remarried a Christian woman called Mary. In my mind, I thought this explained why he was so open to allowing me to pray for my father in Jesus's name when I phoned in from the UK. He was already drawn very close to Christ.

My younger uncle also told me he had been periodically attending a church close to his home. He told me about a powerful witness experience of a Christian woman who employed him as a driver for her family when her husband was very ill and dying. My uncle described how this woman of faith showed him a lot of love and respect and showered him with many gifts even whilst she was going through a very difficult time herself. I was once again amazed and grateful to God for the opportunity to catch glimpses of what God was doing within my extended family. I believe God was sending other people to witness and minister to my family just as I try to do.

That last night with my father was much easier and quite peaceful. Both my half-brother and my uncle are sound sleepers and they slept right through the night. I probably slept one or two hours during the night but I was mostly awake and close to my father.

I spent the night holding his hand, his head, hugging him and talking to him. I was able to pray for him in his ear. Again my most common statement to my father during the night was to repeatedly tell him that 'Jesus loves you' and honestly I must have said this to him a thousand times during the night.

I had to monitor his breathing through the night as sometimes he breathed so heavy and then sometimes the breath went so shallow that I had to examine him to check that he was still actually breathing. I had never been that close to a person about to die but I did not think about what was happening in terms of fear or sadness. I guess I was just happy to be there next to him and to know he had the best chance to make it to heaven.

I must repeat that even at this late stage of his life, my father was not in any obvious pain that I could notice. He sometimes experienced a sort of involuntary jerky movement of his body or limbs, but that was not frequent or excessive in any way. He was still able to hold things in his hands and sometimes he grabbed and pulled my hand or my body towards him as we lay next to each other on the mattress.

The Last Day

Before I recount my father's last day, and in his memory, I want to use these next paragraphs to say a few good things about Islam, the religion he lived all his life practising. To be quite honest, as far as 'religion' goes, Islam as one of the Abrahamic religions is a good one, especially when you think of religion in terms of doctrines of worship and the need to fear and obey God. It is however in my opinion quite deficient when it comes to the person of Jesus Christ and how to obtain eternal life.

Islam requires its followers to pray a minimum of five times a day, from very early in the morning to late at night. This in itself is not a bad principle as many people of faith in the scriptures also have several dedicated times of prayer to God during the day. I read somewhere recently that the Islamic prophet copied the three times a day prayer of the Jews (People of the Book) and then increased it to five times for his followers.

However, what is usually lacking in this form of rigid prayer doctrine and other ritualistic worship is the absence of a loving relationship between

61

God and man, which is only possible through the Lord Jesus Christ. Christianity teaches that man can never perfectly obey all of God's commands and that our righteousness is based on Jesus Christ who came as a man but never sinned and then died for us to pay the price for our sins.

Christians are encouraged to worship God in response to his amazing love for us, which we refer to as the Grace of God. Unfortunately, many modern-day Christians have taken the grace of God to another extreme to think they can ignore God and do whatever they want, only running to Him for help when in deep trouble.

Anyway, the second night turned into morning. It was 5.30 am again and everybody was getting up or being woken up to go to the mosque. My uncle and my half-brother still went even though they were probably not fully convinced. That was great for me as I was again left alone with my father and had another fantastic opportunity to pray for him and to tell him again and again that Jesus loves him so much.

It was time to get him ready for the day when people came back from the mosque. Between me and my half-brother, we washed our father, changed his clothes, sat him up, and fed him. He responded well to prompts to open his mouth and to swallow the food and to take his single tablet. He ate more that morning than he did the previous day, so we were all impressed and thought he was better than the day before.

As we were feeding him, my older sister came into the room and shouted 'look at my father's eyes!' We all looked and there were the wide-open eyes of my father, very bright and clear like a young boy's eyes. We were all quite amazed by what we saw considering that my father had lost his sight for more than two years and had not opened his eyes since. But we did not pay much attention to why and how his eyes were opened so we carried on with feeding him. We gave him his medication, laid him back on the mattress, and made him comfortable. It was around 8.20 am.

My older sister and I had planned to go out that morning to buy her a phone, so I then left my father's room to go and have a shower. As I got out of the shower and was getting dressed, my half-brother came into the room and said 'I think dad is gone'. We both quickly went back to my father's room and there his body laid, lifeless, no more breath, the life was gone out of him and the body was just an empty shell. His doctor happened to arrive just at that time for his morning visit and certified the time of death at 8.45 am on Monday 25th March.

That was it, my earthly father was gone. It feels so surreal even as I write this; my earthly father is gone forever. I think now that my father was dead the moment we laid him down after his breakfast, but it just took my half-brother a while to discover it. Someone, later on, said to us that my father was looking at the angel of death when we saw his eyes wide open. Another person proposed the hypothesis that people get healed of any illness they have just before death and that a blind person's sight will be restored just before they die. Not that any of those beliefs have a bearing on the person's journey after death!

The story of my father's life on earth ended that morning and a new journey began that only he can travel. I have not shed any tears for my father's death and I don't think I will as long as I have the hope that he made it to eternal life in Christ. Rather I will continue to rejoice in the hope that one day we will be together among the multitudes of saints in the worship of our Lord Jesus Christ. But what gave me the hope and confidence that my father got saved in the nick of time? The answer can be found in the completeness of the word of God in the Bible. In my relatively young Christian life, I cannot remember having come across or heard of a situation in which I could not find the right context to illustrate or apply in the written word of God.

The story of the two robbers crucified with Jesus Christ on that first Good Friday described in the three gospels came to my mind and gave me so much hope and comfort at the time of my father's last moments of life on earth. One of them mocked Jesus and asked him to save himself and them but the other rebuked his rogue colleague, recognising his sins as compared to the righteousness of Jesus Christ. The second criminal's last request in Luke 23:42 was 'Jesus remember me when you come into your kingdom' and the Lord answered straight away in Verse 43 'Truly I tell you, today you will be with me in paradise'.

How amazing and awesome is Jesus! A similar request like the one from that criminal can be said in just a few seconds and that is all it takes for anyone else. My father, just like him, did not have the opportunity to be led in the sinner's prayer by any man, he did not get baptised in water or the Holy Spirit to anyone's knowledge, he also did not get the opportunity to live an authentic Christian life on earth. Notwithstanding all these, he had the same opportunity to make it to heaven just like any of us. Hallelujah!

This parable of hope is for everyone who is praying for someone to be saved. Please do not give up praying and interceding for their soul. It only takes a few words to commit to Christ. Those words do not need to be spoken out either as Jesus focuses more on the heart rather than empty words. Remember you may not even be aware the person made their peace with God just before death. Thank you, Jesus!

As for the events that happened after my father's death, there is not much worth recounting in this reflection. As far as I am concerned not one thing that happened after he died is of any significance to my father's eternal life, but that is not what the Muslims believe. To my Muslim relatives, the burial doctrines and the prayer for the dead are very important as they believe it can change the dead's eternal outcome. I, therefore, went along with all the arrangements for burial according to Islamic rights and according to my father's expressed wishes before he stopped talking.

My father was buried the same day he died. Eleven of his twelve surviving children were able to make it to the internment apart from my older brother who had to travel back from the US. He was buried right in front of the house, at a spot he had chosen for himself. His final burial ceremony was quickly arranged for a week after his death. This was basically another big Islamic prayer session with a reception attached at the end. Considering everything that happened I believe the entire family pulled together to give our father a 'befitting' burial.

However, the way the Mullahs behaved on the day my father was buried and his subsequent final burial ceremony was a disgrace to any religion. All of them claimed they were praying for the dead and the relatives but it was very obvious they wanted to rake in as much money as they could during the occasion. I am aware that this is not what all Muslims do but the practice is very common around my father's type of Muslims. Everyone was aware of the exploitation but seemingly agreed with it as if it was the money or the Mullahs that can enable prayers to be answered.

I sat through most of the exploitative prayer sessions in respect of my father but I took several breaks to help me calm down. I hate this practice quite passionately and I let my siblings know but I was also reminded that my father used to do the same as the Mullahs. My Pastor Cousin did better in that he put down some money for prayer and then used the opportunity to preach a minute of truth reminding everyone that all of us will die one day like my father and we ought to all consider our ways.

When I think through everything that happened along my father's journey, I conclude by saying that I believe God did everything on his part to give my father eternal life but my father is the one that had to make the final decision. God extended his life on several occasions to allow him to hear and weigh the gospel. I believe Jesus Christ also appeared to my father in a dream or a vision in answer to the supernatural encounter that we requested. I hope that my father, having met with Jesus Christ, would agree that he made a mistake in following the wrong religion for his entire life and will have committed his life to Jesus.

Emotionally, I was looking for a confirmation that my father made it to heaven but it was not God's plan to reveal that to me at this time. I think I gained some understanding as to this. God is working on me to have more faith and believing Him even when there is no physical evidence. Besides, if I had the confirmation now, there would not be much to look forward to when I think about a future in heaven with both my earthly and my heavenly father. As the Bible clearly states in Hebrews 11:1 'now faith is confidence in what we hope for and assurance about what we do not see'.

I am grateful to God and content in knowing that everything that could have been done from my part was done and most importantly everything required from God's part was done. I know God's heart is to save all mankind including my father but He leaves the final choice to each of us. The ball was certainly in my earthly father's court and only he was allowed to make the final call. I will just cling on the hope of God's love and mercy that my father got home safely.

I will of course also keep on waiting for further revelation from God should he chose to reveal the outcome of the battle for my father's soul. I wonder how God may reveal such knowledge to me and for what purpose? I rarely ever dream as I mentioned and I have never dreamt of any dead person. Still, nothing is impossible for my God.

Apart from the inspiration I got from the death of my father to write this memoir, the experience has also equipped me better in how to minister to people who have lost loved ones. I found that I am more empathetic and understanding when ministering to people going through bereavement and I have come across a few in recent months.

What Is Your Conclusion To Part One?

As I conclude the story of my father's journey, at least for now pending further revelation, I wonder what you as the reader can take out of what you have read so far. What you may call wishful thinking on my part is my hope that my father's story will be an encouragement to you no matter your circumstances, whether you are like me praying and fighting for the souls of your loved ones, or you are the person someone is crying to Jesus to save. I hope you know which side you are on as there is no third category.

If you belong to the latter category, as someone that does not yet know Christ, why don't you open your heart today to know the true God? You can pray to ask the true God to reveal himself to you and I am sure he will. Jesus loves you dearly and he wants you with Him in heaven for eternity but there is only one way and that is through him. 'Jesus is the way the truth and the life and no one can get to the Father except through him' (John 14:6). Please speak to someone today if you are ready to accept Jesus Christ as your personal Lord and Saviour as tomorrow may be too late.

Perhaps you are a Muslim like several of my relatives: why don't you study the Quran for yourself instead of believing what those Mullahs are telling you? Why don't you pray to the God of Abraham, Isaac, and Jacob that you refer to as Allah and ask him to reveal the truth to you? Do you know that the Quran records the virgin birth of Jesus, that a whole chapter of the Quran was dedicated to Maryam the mother of Jesus? Do you know that Mary is the only female mentioned by name in the Quran and that she was mentioned more in the Quran than in the New Testament Bible?

Do you know that Jesus (Issah) was given the greatest prominence as a prophet and the name Jesus was explicitly mentioned about twenty-five times in the Quran excluding when he was referred to as the Messiah[7]? Mohammed is explicitly mentioned by name only about five times. Do you know the Quran stated that Jesus will come back before judgement day to defeat the anti-Christ[8] and bring peace to the world?

My brothers and sisters in Islam, do you know that there is more that unites Muslims and Christians than separates us? Do you know that Mohammed even told Muslims to be closest to Christians as they are good people? If you are a

Muslim, you are already closer to Christ and his gift of salvation than you think.

But some truths separate Christianity from Islam and these are what every Muslim must overcome. You have to believe in the divinity and supremacy of Jesus, that he is truly the son of God and God Himself. You have to believe in his miraculous birth through the Holy Spirit, his sinless life on earth, his death to pay for your sins, and His resurrection from death to life. You have to believe the fact that it is only through Jesus Christ that you can be reconciled to God. Are you at a point in your life where you want to know the truth and receive the gift of salvation from Jesus?

All you need to do is to pray the following prayer to God in whatever way or language you can, as long as you are sincere. First, you must accept that you are a sinner and that you can never be perfect no matter how hard you try. Then you need to accept Jesus Christ as God, your Lord, and Saviour and ask Him to forgive all of your sins. You must tell Jesus that you believe he already died for your sins and that he rose again from the dead after three days to demonstrate to you that he will raise you from the dead to live in eternity with him. Then ask Jesus to come into your life and help you by His Holy Spirit so that you can now live a life of obedience to him.

My brothers and sisters, if you have prayed the above prayer, you are born again and have received the gift of eternal life. Congratulations and welcome to your new life in Christ! Make sure you tell someone you trust who will link you to a Bible-believing Church so you can start to live the transformed life of a child of God.

If you are in my kind of situation, still praying for your loved ones to be saved, I plead with you in the name of our Lord Jesus Christ not to give up hope. He is mighty enough to save anyone no matter how far they seem to be away from God and their salvation needs just a few seconds to happen. As long as that person is alive, do not stop praying and interceding for their soul to be saved. Keep fighting for the eternal life of your loved ones and seek to be strengthened in your inner being (Ephesians 3: 14-21) so you can remain on the battlefield to the end.

Lastly, I want to encourage those of us who still have a sense of guilt over loved ones who have died and for whom we feel we did not fight enough for their salvation. I have personal experience of this because I lost a very good friend twenty-six years ago when I was not even saved myself. That death is probably still the most traumatic experience I've had. The medical team in the hospital he was in told us there is not much anyone could do and they encouraged us to simply go and pray. I was unable to say a single prayer, whether for healing or salvation for my friend, simply because I did not have a relationship with God. I lived with that guilt for a very long time.

The truth is that we cannot change what has already happened; only God can do so. This same God is very willing to forgive and forget our mistakes if we only ask, repent, and resolve to do better in the future. Each day is an opportunity for a new beginning and so we can always aim to do better. Another way to look at this is that we may never really know if someone eventually got saved before they die, bearing in mind that some salvation takes just a few seconds. Why blame yourself for something you are not responsible for? Why lose your joy or even your salvation for someone who already made it to heaven? I pray for you in the name of Jesus that you will overcome any guilt over things of the past and that you will be able to do better going forward.

If you are in my kind of position I pray for you as I continue to pray for myself, in the name of our Lord Jesus Christ: 'that out of His glorious riches He may strengthen you with power through His Spirit in your inner being, so that Christ may dwell in your hearts through faith. And I pray that you, being rooted and established in love, may have power, together with all the Lord's holy people, to grasp how wide and long and high and deep is the love of Christ, and to know this love that surpasses knowledge—that you may be filled to the measure of all the fullness of God. Now to him who can do immeasurably more than all we ask or imagine, according to his power that is at work within us, to him be glory in the church and in Christ Jesus throughout all generations, for ever and ever! Amen' (Ephesians 3:16-21).

PART TWO

My Testimony Of Salvation

It took me many years to find Jesus and accept Him as my Lord and Saviour. This is because my childhood and youthful years were used in resisting and rebelling against the religion of my family (Islam). I also rebelled against all 'authorities'. I did so many things at that time of my life that I am not proud of. Many evangelists shared the Gospel of the Lord Jesus Christ with me but my mind was hardened and I refused to listen.

My life started to change and my rebellious stance was challenged during my late twenties when a vision began to be revealed to me year after year. In these dreams, I saw the vision of the Lord Jesus Christ coming to gather the believers but I was left behind. In these 'nightmares' I experienced the unimaginable and unbearable regret of missing out on the most anticipated and joyous moment in mankind's history. Those visions finally persuaded me to make the prayer to give my life to the Lord Jesus Christ and to accept Him as my personal Lord and Saviour.

I have been saved by the power of love from Jesus Christ who left His heavenly place to come to this world to suffer and be crucified for my sins. I do not have to rebel anymore because every act of worship from me is joyful obedience to someone who gave everything for me on the Cross of Calvary. As Jesus said in John 14:23: 'Anyone who loves me will obey my teaching. My Father will love them, and we will come to them and make our home with them'.

Accepting Jesus Christ into my life has turned it around completely. Sin no longer has power over me and I now rejoice daily for my salvation and my redemption. I have since received confirmation in the most joyous vision I ever had when Jesus came down from Heaven and I was among the chosen ones. I now know for certain that my name is written in the book of life because of the conscious decision I made to accept Jesus into my life.

Jesus Christ knocked on the door to my heart through the visions of his second coming and I am so grateful that I had that experience. I believe that Jesus is knocking on your door as well but maybe in different ways?

You can also have the same assurance of your heavenly place. All you have to do is open your heart and accept the Lord Jesus Christ as your personal Lord and Saviour, repent of your sins and he will do the rest for you. Every one of us is free to make this choice and we will all individually answer for the decision we make. Please don't leave your decision for another day because nobody knows when it will be too late.

If this testimony strikes a resonance with you and you also want to invite Jesus into your life, please say the following prayer:

Dear God in heaven, I come to you in the name of Jesus. I acknowledge to you that I am a sinner, and I am sorry for my sins and the life that I have lived. I need your forgiveness.

I believe that your only begotten Son Jesus Christ shed his precious blood on the Cross at Calvary and died for my sins, and I am now willing to turn from my sin.

I believe that Jesus rose again to life on the third day and he can raise me also on the last day.

This very moment I accept Jesus Christ as my personal Saviour and according to his word, right now I am saved.

Thank you, Jesus, for dying for me and giving me eternal life. Please fill me with your Holy Spirit so I can live the new life you have given me.
Amen.

Am I A Reflection Of My Father?

What I will be sharing in the next few chapters is how I believe my new faith came to be. But to start with, I would like to reflect a little bit on the relationship with my earthy father.

Good or bad, present or absent, we all feel the impact our earthly fathers leave in our lives. 'Each of us grows up with a common longing and a deep-seated need for a father's love, support, acceptance, security, and presence in our lives. Sadly, for many, this need is not met, or only partially fulfilled by an earthly dad. As a result, some unknowingly transfer negative perceptions of fathers into their relationships with God. Yet, God longs to be known as a Perfect Father. Through Jesus Christ, this relationship is available to everyone. Through spiritual birth, we all can see, know, and enjoy God as a Perfect Father'. A quote from *Not Forsaken: Finding Freedom as Sons and Daughters of a Perfect Father* by Louie Giglio.

What I loved most about my father was his open-mindedness as he demonstrated personally to me that he was able to listen to other views of religion and faith. I was impressed when I learnt that my father was actively involved in inter-faith discussion forums in his younger days. In the last few years of his life, he was able to discuss with me the principles of the Christian faith and the person of Jesus Christ. He accepted to be prayed for in the name of Jesus and he testified to the healing power of Jesus during my last family visit to him.

I loved my father's eagerness to learn and his passion to teach others; indeed he was an educator to the core and he loved to impart knowledge to people around him. I loved his fun lifestyle, his jokes in an attempt to bring smiles to everyone's faces. I also loved his ability to relate with people of different ages, backgrounds, cultures, or social standing.

Bearing in mind that no one is perfect, one major mistake I believe my father made in his life was marrying more than one wife. It took me many years to forgive him for this mistake and what I saw as the preferential good treatment he gave to my step-mother and my half-siblings. The next character flaw I saw was his over-generosity to others which sometimes crossed boundaries and effectively caused harm to him and those he was trying to help. A common analogy of this is constantly giving someone 'fish' instead of investing in them so that they can 'catch fish' for themselves.

As I write this I remember a strange old man said to me many years ago when I was a little child 'you are exactly like your father'. This person was referring to physical resemblance as he did not even know me, but I have grown to realise that I inherited all the good and the bad characteristics of my earthly father too. This is good for me to know so I can consciously cultivate the good and ask the Holy Spirit to help me overcome the bad. I have to continuously pray against the generational bad traits that run through families so that I can protect myself and generations to come.

I realise I have already made a few of the mistakes I saw in my father before I got saved, but thankfully not the most serious ones. I have narrowly escaped making one or two of the serious flaws of judgement and I am aware that I am prone to make similar mistakes in the future. I have also come to realise as my father did late in his life, that God has given me a wife to complement me. My wife is a tower of strength in those areas where I am weak; just as my mother was to my father, I need to learn from that and keep growing in listening more and valuing her support.

However, I have also learnt that the bad human characteristics referred to as the old self did not just come from my father, but originated from

Adam and Eve who were the first humans to disobey God. I have to constantly remind myself that the new self in me was created to be like God in true righteousness and holiness. I have to always be vigilant to examine my motive at all times to recognise any hidden evil and ask for God's help to get rid of it whenever it raises its head. I have to make a daily choice about which father to follow and to always obey my perfect heavenly Father.

Early Childhood

Thankfully I have very few childhood memories so hopefully, you will not be bored with a lot of rambling about nothing! Also, either my relatives are not good storytellers or maybe I don't sit around them long enough or forget what they have told me. There was also the disadvantage of the unavailability of recording devices such as photographs and videos in those days which limits what could have been recorded - now that is making me feel old!

I was born on 16th April 1970 in a town where my father settled and was living with his two wives at the time. My father by then had two daughters and a son through my mother and another son who was born by my step-mother six months before me. I was never allowed to forget this half-brother was six months older than me as that automatically gave him the first choice in everything!

My mother was still in the hospital when I was named on the 7th day. This only came to my knowledge because one person said almost accusingly to me at one time, 'Is this not the boy who when we were naming him his mother was in the hospital?' My mother then confirmed it. I never really found out what kept my mother in the hospital or sent her back to the hospital, but that knowledge made me love her more and also feel guilty for sending her to the hospital.

I remember my father as a rich man in those days. He was one of the few who were educated in the area, he was running a successful business and we owned the only television set for miles around. Our house was therefore always full of neighbours coming to watch TV. We also always had relatives who were either staying permanently with us or had come for a visit.

We initially lived in a two-bedroom bungalow within a compound and later on my father also rented a room and parlour (sitting room) within the same compound. My mother and my step-mother had a room each and all of us children slept together on the floor of the living room. I could remember periods when up to ten children would sleep on mats there. Sometimes the mornings got interesting when trying to work out which of the children had wet the mat so to speak! Some young children were clever enough to change the spot where they slept at night but sometimes the urine just flowed across the floor and made everyone guilty!

For some reason, in those days the ability to touch one's ear from the other side of the head was used as a sign of readiness to start primary school. I don't think it was anything to do with the child's age as we all had birth certificates to show our age at the time. I remember my first attempt to enter primary school failed because of two things, firstly my hand could not reach my ear on the other side of my head, and secondly, my voice was not strong enough. This meant I had to try again the following year and luckily I made it that time, possibly because I had grown and my hand was long enough. My voice, unfortunately, has never really got strong enough to shout.

I remember having to repeat my year three in primary school because I had an appendectomy that kept me in hospital for months. I still can't understand how having such a minor operation could have taken so long. In the end, the repeat of year three worked well for me as I remember that I became a clever and intelligent pupil once I returned to school. I still have the scar from the appendectomy so it was certainly not brain surgery! I then started coming either first or second in the class after every end of term examinations. I supposed that the two years that I had somehow lost and gained due to delayed entry to primary school and the appendectomy meant that I was better positioned to learn than my classmates.

There was a funny or more accurately an embarrassing story about my father's attendance at a parents' association meeting when he stood up at the end and promised the school some fridges for our Home Economics class. Everybody was excited about this promise as a fridge was not easy to come about in those days. I was the school golden for a few days until my father showed up with his promised fridges. What the school did not hear within the pledge was that my father promised 'traditional fridges'. This only became obvious when my father arrived in school with large clay pots instead of the shiny electric or gas fridges the school was expecting.

Apart from the above moment of embarrassment, primary school was really fun as far as I could remember although I think I must have been too quiet to make any lasting friendships. There is only one boy I remember from school and that is probably because he was an albino and so difficult to forget. I can even remember his name. The only girl I vaguely remember was the girl I was left to partner with on the day of our final school disco. The class teacher asked every boy to choose a girl partner and it was only me and the girl left at the end. I supposed I was a slow learner in the social things as well but I certainly made up for it in my adolescent years. Also, the fact I left this town after my primary schooling did not help in maintaining any sort of relationship.

My Early Impression Of Islam

My parents and relatives have always described Islam as a religion of peace and total submission to Allah. I will leave you to form your own opinion on whether Islam is a religion of peace in the context of the number of 'Muslims' with the ideology to conquer the world for Allah by violence and terror. It is the notion of total submission to Allah because of fear and without questioning (by the interpretation of the so-called Mullahs) that I struggled with right from childhood and this made me quickly rebel against the religion as soon as I was able to make any decision for myself.

I am going to write about a few of the specific issues that I dislike in the way Islam was portrayed to me. But I think the core of the matter is that I don't like to be told to do anything, I like to be treated with love and compassion and I like people to take the time to explain things to me. I have always seen myself as an independent thinker who can consider the information available and I like to be able to make up my mind.

Going to the Quranic School as a young child was a bad experience. We used to go to a group class in the afternoon where we learnt to read Arabic from wooden slates and later on we graduated to the paper version. The teacher, if I can call him that, was cruel and did not pay attention to what we were learning.

All I remembered him do was lift his long horsetail whip at regular intervals to thrash out in any area where he was not getting the right volume of noise. The trick then for us was to shout out the readings when we see his hands going for the whip. But there was no way to escape the whip as it would get you at some point during the lesson. Everything we managed to learn was in Arabic, reciting, and memorising the text with no interpretation or explanation.

Being taught at home was much better academically as we received more or less 1:1 tuition from an uncle who came to live with us. But the cruelty from this uncle to us children is probably the biggest contributing factor to my dislike of the Islamic religion. Now, this uncle was not your usual Mullah with no education or a real job. This was a well-educated man who worked with one of the few multi-national companies in existence in the town at that time. He used to dress smartly in western clothes - well-tailored and ironed trousers, shirts, and tie, and he even rode a shiny brand new motorbike!

This was the uncle to whom our father entrusted our Arabic learning and discipline and I must say he did a good job of both. He devoted a lot of his time to teaching us the Arabic alphabets, to reading and memorising a big chunk of the Quran. However, he was merciless and he punished us for every wrong he caught us (or suspected us) of doing. Our offence could range from not reading, not praying, playing football, not waking up on time, coming home late from school, and so on. The punishments were harsh corporal punishments and that is the only way I can describe them.

This uncle managed to invent a painful art of torture in waking up a child from sleep for prayers which he did by striking an open can on to the top shoulder of the child (warning – please do not try this on any person!). I can still now remember the pain of this experience as I write, and an open can now hold a different meaning to me.

But I wasn't just going to take all of this abuse from my uncle without getting some revenge! So one day I got a razor blade and cut through all his nice western clothes where he used to hang them. He was so pained over this destruction. But unfortunately, though I had achieved the desired effect my revenge was blamed on my half-brother and he got a lot of punishment for something he did not do. I must remember to confess this to both my uncle and half-brother and ask for their forgiveness. I have already confessed to God and asked for His.

But it is interesting how my half-brother got blamed! My father, even though he was a committed Muslim, still dealt in some pagan practices like fortune-telling or casting lots. It was one of these techniques he used to try and find out who used the razor to cut my uncle's clothes which unfortunately identified my half-brother as the culprit. The good early learning for me there was to recognise those lots castings don't work!

It seems the razor was my weapon of choice in getting back at people then, or perhaps acquired learning based on one successful application. I used the razor again sometime later to cut the tarpaulin cover of someone's vehicle. This time it was a neighbour who punished me among other children for an offence I cannot remember now. But in those days it was common for a neighbour or any random adult or older child to punish you there and then for offences committed without referring you to your parents. It was likely you would get another round of punishment when one's parents got to know about it.

Anyway, I was caught in the act of shredding this neighbour's vehicle cover and received a serious beating from my parents. That was the end of my use of razors. For me, the good outcome was that the neighbour never again raised his hands to beat me. He more or less ignored me for the rest of my time living in that compound.

This cruel and abusive experience mostly from my uncle turned out to be good for me in a way because it is partly what made me rebel against Islam from childhood. This made it possible for me to find it easy to break out of the Islamic religion but it also made me run away from God or anything religious for a long time. I saw my Islamic teacher uncle again on the last journey to see my father and I thank God for giving me the grace to forgive him for what he did to me in the past. I also thank God for the new me as I no longer have the urge to seek revenge when people hurt me.

The other person I think of as I reflect on the Muslim early morning prayers is my mother. She is a different personality to my uncle and she used a different approach to bring my attention to important things. She used to refuse to say good morning or acknowledge me in the morning until I had been to the mosque for prayers.

My mother knew me well enough to know that her not talking to me would get my attention as I am more affected by emotional suffering than physical. She tried her other approach of withholding food until you obey, but that was nothing to me as I never really liked food and I could go without for a long time even as a child. One of my nicknames as a child can be translated as 'the person who has a mouth but does not eat'.

I supposed what my mother was trying to communicate was that our relationship with God is more important than our relationship with each other which is great but I don't think she managed to communicate that well enough.

I am thankful to God that my mother nowadays can relate to me even though she knows I am now a Christian. She does not now try to make me follow her religion, she says good morning to me even if I have not been to the mosque, she even recently wished me happy resurrection day when I spoke to her on Easter Sunday!

Teenage Troubles

Apart from a few major rebellious acts, I was still less troublesome than most kids around me until I became a teenager, then all hell broke loose. My teenage years were probably the most significant in terms of my character formation and my perception of life. Most of my lasting friendships were formed at this stage.

So having escaped the threat of going to wholly Islamic education, I relocated to live and attend a secondary school in a university community, with my eldest sister who was also a teacher, forming friends with children of university academicians, and having my room in a separate building to the main house known as 'Boys' Quarters'.

I came twenty-first in the class in my first term in secondary school which was a shock to me as I was used to coming first or second in my primary school. But I quickly realised that I had been a local champion, that this was now a university community and the standard was much higher. I quickly re-adjusted and recovered from the temporary setback and by the end of the second term, I was back to being in the first or second position.

I may also have received some motivation from my sister who promised to buy me a bicycle if my position in class improved. But unfortunately, that promise was never fulfilled for some reason. I must also say that my sister being a teacher in the school helped me to behave myself there for at least a couple of years before things got out of hand.

In terms of practising of Islam, the fact that I had my private quarters meant that I could escape the group prayers. I could still go with my sister for the weekly Jumat service or pretend that I was fasting during the month of Ramadan but I could easily get out of doing most of the Islamic rituals.

My sister tried her best to raise me properly and to monitor my behaviour but there was not much she could do really to contain how I was growing up. I was rebellious to all authorities at home and in school. My sister tried to punish and discipline me but that didn't have a positive effect. For example, there was a time when she said every minute I came home late from school was a stroke of cane on the back of my leg. That did not stop me from coming home whenever I pleased. My late homecomings increased to an extent her hands would get tired from beating me, they stopped having any impact and she just had to stop them.

My sister would check in the morning that I was wearing the proper and agreed school uniforms such as brown sandals, my shirt tucked in, and my collar in the right position. By the time I stepped out of her car in school, everything would have changed. By then I would have ditched my sandals to shoes or trainers, my shirt would be hanging out of my shorts and I was decked in jewellery like the bad boys of those days.

My behaviour must have been a total embarrassment for my poor sister as a teacher in the school and it was only recently that I apologised to her for all the grief I caused when I was living with her. She left my school to go and teach in another when I was in year three, probably to save herself from further embarrassment, but then my behaviour escalated even more. I joined every bad group that was available, latecomers, smokers, drinkers, missing classes, missing school, and so on.

All of this escalating rebellious behaviour was happening around the time when Colonel Gaddaffi of Libya was standing up to President Ronald Reagan of the United States hence my mathematics teacher then nicknamed me 'Gaddaffi'. This name stuck with me for a long time; there are still some people who don't know me by any other name. Most of my long-term friends were acquired at this time of my life and they introduced me to their parents and later their children as Gaddaffi.

Strangely enough, even with all the trouble, I was causing in school my academic performance did not suffer too much. I dropped further mathematics because the teacher failed me in one test and later on I dropped geography because the teacher beat students whose notes were not up to date and I knew mine would never be. But I maintained my position of coming second in the class for most of the class exams.

I was almost expelled at the latter end of my final year in school because of a serious altercation I had with the school principal which was witnessed by most people in school. A group of us were found messing about in the forest when we should be learning in class. We were all taken to the principal to receive our due punishment which was to receive a beating from the cane. Well, I took the cane off him, broke it into pieces, and loudly called him abusive names as I walked out of his office and out of school, witnessed by many other pupils!

It took my sister's intervention to get the school to allow me to take my GSCE exams. Even then I was suspended for the last two weeks before the exam and I still had to go to school to serve a corporal punishment of filling potholes on the road leading to the school. Despite all this, I came second in the overall results for the school with distinctions in all seven subjects I took. Imagine how much better I would have done if I had focused more on my education!

Thank God that I did well in my GCSEs because that was the only reason I think my sister agreed to continue looking after me. She had sent me packing back to my mother straight after the exams because I was just too much trouble for her. But she later gave me a chance to get a university education. My family wanted me to become a medical doctor as we already had a pharmacist and a lawyer in the family but I didn't care about education. I used to say it doesn't matter what I study, I am just going to go and make good money. I didn't have a plan on how to make the money but it did cross my mind that I would like to marry into big money.

Anyway, after about two years of pretending to try to pass the entrance examination to medical school, in which I did not try to be honest, I was allowed to go and study chemistry at the university to cross over to medicine in the second year. But that was my relatives' hope, not mine. As far as I was concerned my going to university was just passing time until I could make big money. I ended up studying chemistry for seven years up to the master's degree level, still waiting for the opportunity to get rich.

Early Adulthood

If my secondary school and teenage years were rebellious, my university and early adulthood was great fun as I had the freedom to do anything I wanted. I mean, one can only rebel if there is something to fight against and I was mostly out of my family's control in the university. I lived in the hostel on campus or at one stage a private rented accommodation out of campus. I had enough money to live well because by then my older brother and sister were based in the United States and were sponsoring my education. I had friends who became more like family to me and sometimes I chose not to go home during the holidays, preferring to stay in on the campus or go with my friends.

The academic side of my university life was not eventful. I did not mix much with the class and I only did the minimum required to pass the course. I can't say I enjoyed it either as I was not interested in university education or chemistry for that matter. I missed a lot of classes but I always just managed to get by doing what I needed to do to move to the next level.

There were specific bad things that I did or was involved in from my secondary school and my university days which I cannot write openly about for personal reasons and the protection of others. I can, however, say that I was loyal to my friends and I tried to see the greater good in everything I was doing. For example, I joined a society on campus that was like a vigilante group to protect the innocent when gangs and cult attacks were becoming rampant. I could have easily joined the cults based on my reputation but I chose to be on the side of the innocent majority.

From just after my secondary school days, and together with few close friends, we formed a group known as De Hard Family with the sole aim of supporting and standing with each other no matter what situation we found ourselves in. This group grew from three to nine and became international when some of us travelled abroad. I eventually took myself out of this group a year after I accepted Christ as my Lord and Saviour.

Two of the original people in this group have since died, one of whom was a strong Brother in the Lord. We used to call him Colonel but he died being known as Pastor. He prophesied that I would fulfil my dream of living abroad long before the dream was achieved. I thank God that all of us remaining alive from the group are now following Christ apart from one person that I am not sure about. We expelled him from our group because he joined a different organisation that we knew was evil. I am grateful to God for the opportunity to have led one of the group members in the prayer to accept Jesus Christ into his life as Lord and Saviour.

Talking about people dying, the most traumatic experience I had was when my younger brother and my closest friend at university died within three months of each other. What pained me about my late brother's death was that I felt he did not deserve to die at that age and in the circumstances it happened. As far as I knew he was a well-behaved, respectful, honest, God-fearing, and prayerful boy. But for some reason that only God knows, his life was cut short at the tender age of 19. I was really sad about my brother's death but also very angry that I was not told about his sickness and death. My anger was based on pride as there was nothing I could have done at that time to help my brother.

I still grieve the death of my younger brother for a number of reasons. To start with, most of the decisions in his life were made for him by others, most especially his religion and education and he seemed to me like a person who did not deserve anything bad to happen to him.

His death was shrouded in secrecy and up till now, I do not know the full circumstances surrounding it. But I can guess some unpleasant incidents took place before his death and he probably showed some evidence of mental illness which the family tried to cover up. The explanation I was provided with as to why I wasn't informed he was ill was that the decision was made to protect me as I was in university at the time and preparing for an exam.

My very close friend, who was like my twin brother, was the one who consoled me after I eventually learnt about my brother's death and he then also died three months later. He had a stomach ulcer that he had been managing since I knew him but his death came very quickly after complaining of stomach ache and he ended up in a hospital. Before anyone knew what was going on my friend was in a critical condition and he passed away within a couple of weeks in the hospital.

My friend's death came when I was with him in the hospital. He could not talk anymore by that time. I saw tears in his eyes for some reason I do not know up until today. He probably did not want to die or perhaps there was something he wanted to tell me but he could not communicate. Were they tears of pity for me that I was going to be alone without him? Were they tears of pleading for me to do something for him? Your guess is as good as mine. Suddenly my friend started gasping for breath and we shouted for help.

The doctors came around and then sent us out of the ward saying there was nothing more we could do but to go and pray for him. I went outside the ward, knelt by a bench but no single prayer could be formed in my heart or my mouth. I realised I wasn't a Muslim, I wasn't a Christian, I did not know any supernatural being to pray to and ask for help for my friend. But my heart was so hardened at that time that I did not get the significance of not being able to intercede for my best friend. On reflection, that incident remains the second most significant regret of my life and I still hurt when I think about it.

The most significant regret of my life so far is my lateness in accepting Jesus Christ as my personal Lord and Saviour. I only got to accept the grace and love of Christ after 40 years. But I know my God is a redeemer and there is nothing impossible for him. So I am trusting that God will allow me the opportunity to achieve everything he has for me to do in this world even though I was late in coming on board.

The cause of death on my friend's death certificate was recorded as 'enterocolitis mellitus'. I don't know if any prayer could have saved him and most importantly I don't know if he was saved in Christ. I wasn't saved at the time and we did not have any serious conversations about faith. My regret is mainly that I should have been in a position to intercede for my friend when he was incapable of doing anything for himself. I wasn't. I have asked God to forgive me and also wash me clean from the guilt. I have repented and my resolve is that by God's grace that kind of failure will not happen to me again. As long as I have breath within me, I will use it to cry to the Lord and intercede for people around me, especially for salvation for their eternal souls.

Jesus Is Calling – The Awakening

I never really knew anything about Christianity when I was a child. Although the town had a predominantly Muslim population, we still had a few Christians living in the same compound with us. All I remember about those Christians was them giving us special food they cooked at Christmas and Easter. That special food was the prestigious white rice with stew and chicken. We did the same for them during Muslim festivals and that was as far as an exchange of faith went.

As I got my freedom from Islam during my secondary school and teenage years, I started hearing a bit here and there about Christianity. The university campus and the town had more Christians than Muslims as far as I could tell. My friends were mostly from Christian families but I had no religious friends at that time. Some churches came into existence which were more evangelistic in approach. We used to refer to all those evangelists as Deeper Life people but they probably came from other Pentecostal Churches as well.

I must have had several encounters with those evangelists right through my secondary school and university days. But I never gave them or their message any great thought. We used to make fun of them all the time. There was a particular boy who pestered us so much that one day we decided to give him a chance and invited him to my friend's house for a chat. I cannot remember anything he said as we were not listening. Then he asked us to join hands together and pray.

Very happy that we gave him the opportunity, he closed his eyes and promptly started to pray. My friend and I were just giggling and then we started making 'breakdance' moves with our body. Our movements seemed to energise our evangelist even more as he started praying more vigorously whilst we kept giggling and dancing away! I can still now see his face filled with sadness and disappointment when he opened his eyes and realised what was going on.

I wish I know where my evangelist is now so I could go and give him a big hug! I wish I could apologise to him and offer to compensate him for what I did. I wish he could know that the bad boy he prayed for that time is now a changed man and trying to follow in his footsteps. I hope he had faith that his prayers were going to be answered and I hope that he is still out there trying to bring people into the kingdom of God.

What I know is that I have repented of this sin and the Good Father has forgiven me just like many others. I know that I am going to spend the rest of my life making up for that callous and evil behaviour. I also know that by using myself as an example to never give up hope on anyone no matter how they react to my sharing of the gospel with them.

The second notable evangelist encounter was just after my friend died. This time it was a random street evangelist who came to me whilst on campus and started talking to me about Christ. I remember where this encounter took place as it was the entrance to the female hostel I used to frequent. The only statement I remembered from this encounter was this person saying 'they threw one stone, it landed behind you, they threw another it landed beside you, don't you realise the next one may get you?'

This evangelist probably had prophetic gifting as we did not know each other and I immediately recognised he was referring to my brother and friend's death. Did I pay any attention to him? No! My heart was so hardened I was ready to die rather than accept Jesus. Why did the third stone not land on me? Was it never thrown or did someone intercede for me and the Father showed mercy? These are more answers that will be revealed when Christ is fully revealed to me. What I now know is that God saved me from certain death for His purpose to be done through me, one of which is so you can read about my story in this book.

My heart was so hardened that Jesus himself had to come and reveal himself to me, even more so He had to come many times until I said yes to Him. But He did not give up on me and I am so grateful.

Jesus Is Calling - Personal Encounter

I am aware that people dream a lot in my family. I also know that dreaming has been a precursor to mental health breakdowns in at least one member of the family. So I was naturally afraid of dreams. I smoked cigarettes at least once every night for about twenty-five years of my life based on the false belief that a cigarette will put me off into a deep sleep so I wouldn't dream.

I did not remember most of my dreams up until when I finished my first degree at the age of twenty-five. What I used to have then was the weird feeling that 'I have been here before' when certain things happen. As such things started unfolding I could almost predict the sequence of what was going to happen next. This made me think that I had dreamt of the incident before and only just remembering it as it was unfolding. Thankfully this does not happen anymore and a different set of dreams started when I finished my first degree.

This episode started when I went to complete what is known as the National Youth Service, in a far and remote part of the country. I was still living my careless, uncaring, and godless lifestyle.

The village I was posted to was lifeless with little to do so I spent a lot of time indoors, and it was too hot to sleep. As God would have it, a former occupant of my room had left a Bible in there. I picked it up with the sole intention of finding evidence that I could use to challenge those notorious evangelists if I should come across another one.

I took a notebook and a pen and I diligently read through that Bible from the first page to the last. I took copious notes of what I took as evidence to be used in my next debate with anyone who would dare talk to me about Christianity. Interestingly, I did not take this approach with Islam or the Quran. I was totally off the Islamic religion for the reasons I have already cited.

Also, another big reason I knew Islam was not for me anymore was that I knew that I could never rigidly follow a legalistic set of rules that would be my only way to get to heaven. Even then I would not be sure as I would be hoping that Allah would forgive any minor mistakes I made along the way. A Muslim never knows whether he has done enough to earn a place in paradise unless, as a false ideology used to recruit terrorists, he goes to his death by martyrdom. The way Christianity was presented to me was different and I saw something was compelling about the gospel that I had to do something to counteract. It seemed like Christianity was a threat to my way of life at the time as I realised I would not be able to continue my sinful way of life that I enjoyed at the time if I don't find a way to refute the gospel.

So my notebook was filled with extracts from the Bible, of course, taken out of context, so that they could be used to justify my sinful lifestyle and general bad behaviour. For example the word of God in Genesis 2:18 that 'it is not good for the man to be alone' was my justification for having a girlfriend all the time; Jesus turning water to wine was a licence for me to continue my alcohol abuse. Jesus's statement in Matthew 15:24 about him sent only to the lost sheep of Israel was my excuse that I was not among those who Jesus came to save. Jesus's response to my compilation of erroneous evidence against his gospel was to show himself directly to me.

I had my first nightmare just after I finished reading the Bible. I had the same, or more or less the same vision, at least once, but sometimes twice a year, every year for the next fifteen years. Even before I describe this vision I must warn you that my words cannot do justice to what I saw in the vision. Perhaps if I was an artist I could draw it better but I doubt even if a drawing could accurately depict such an experience.

Each started the same way in the sense that I would immediately recognise what was about to happen just before it did. This is similar to as I described before about a dream becoming a reality as the event started to unfold. There would be a loud noise followed immediately by a heavy silence. Wherever I was I would immediately look into the sky, with my heart beating very fast, my body going limp, sweat breaking out from all pores of my body. Fear, despair, sadness, desperation, helplessness, and hopelessness were the feelings that immediately started to feed on my soul.

I looked up and my fear was confirmed. Coming down from the cloud in full view of the entire world was Jesus. He did not need any introduction even though a host of angels were coming down with him. He was always at the forefront, riding on a white horse. And the brilliance of the entourage was blinding and indescribable. But you know what; I could never keep my head up long enough to capture the beauty of it all.

I would fall face down as if struck by lightning, in pure agony, crying rivers of tears, incapable of movement, or anything else. I could sense the pandemonium around me as people were running around and screaming. The aftermath was seeing my miserable and lost self wandering around, sometimes in a wilderness, walking around for days, crying, sorrowful, hopeless, regretting why I let this happen to me. Why did I not accept Jesus when I had the chance, why was my heart so hard, what did I have to lose?

The aftermath of the vision only lasted a day or two and then I would go back to my usual self, and life went on as normal until the next nightmare.

The Transition Years

The first person I told about my vision of the second coming of Jesus Christ was a cousin who died may years ago now. I don't know how or why the conversation came about but I think we were both drunk and uninhibited at that time. He was of course not a practising Muslim and we were together engaged in all sorts of bad behaviour. I think sometimes that my telling my cousin about my nightmare could be the only gospel he heard before he died and I was not even saved myself then. Anyway, I did not tell another relative until many years later.

I have had to reflect on why it took me so long to accept Jesus Christ as my personal Lord and Saviour. Jesus appeared to have used two significant means that can touch me. The first was the 'dreams'.

The second significant factor is emotional pain. My heart was hardened to any physical sort of pain, and I would gladly receive a hundred lashes instead of seeing someone I love refuse to say hello to me. I am very emotionally wired and I think a lot. So there was an aftermath of emotional pain which I experienced each time Jesus came in those nightmares. The pain of knowing I was lost was just indescribable. If anything was going to make me think about the afterlife, it was the fear of emotional torment for eternity. Yet it took me fifteen years to finally accept the gift of salvation.

From what I have read and seen around the world about Muslims who have converted to Christianity and using myself as a case study, I can say I have some understanding of how difficult it is for someone from a strong Islamic background to accept Jesus Christ as their Lord and Saviour. This is equally applicable whether the person is a devout practising Muslim or a Muslim by heritage as I was. My impression is that majority of Muslims are in a kind of spiritual darkness that requires the experience of supernatural encounters with Jesus through dreams, visions, miraculous interventions, or healing before they can be born again.

This is because, in my experience, the Islamic religion is steeped in dogmatic followership and people are indoctrinated not to question their faith or the authenticity of the Quran or the interpretation of Islamic Scholars. This can be easily illustrated by what is happening in Islamic caliphates where a ruler will have supreme power and be able to dictate to everyone. The freedom we have in the western world is another reason why Islamic fundamentalists hate us and want to make everywhere the Islamic state. I am someone that loves the freedom of expression so my experience of dogmatic followership already made me dislike Islam, but it also made me hate all religions as I was of the view they were all the same.

Another major factor that could prevent freedom from Islam is the physical danger, intimidation, and relationship trauma that is likely to arise as a result of a Muslim's conversion to Christianity. There was never a time I felt I would be in physical danger from my Muslim relatives and I was not afraid that anyone could intimidate me. But the trauma of the hurt and shame I thought I was going to cause my relatives, especially my parents, was part of the reason I ignored the Lord's calling on my life for very many years.

For me, it was a straight choice between what I will gain as a Christian versus the hurt and pain I was going to cause my relatives. The few days of emotional torment I experienced once or twice a year in the nightmares did not seem enough to cause all the likely pain to my parents. But that was Satan's plan, for me to only think about earthly pleasure instead of eternity implication of the choice.

Selfishly I was also solely dependent on my family. It would have been a financial struggle for me then if my siblings decided to stop paying my way. Another potential loss for me would have been the loss of relationship with my relatives. I currently know of at least two close relatives who are in the same situation, and my prayer is that my story will inspire them to know they can also let others know they have chosen to accept Jesus Christ as their personal Lord and Saviour.

I thank God for the amazing testimony I have and the many examples of people who have managed to break out of Islam into the Kingdom of Christ. The determination of these converts to face the threat of persecution, including even death and the obvious transformation for good in the lives of such converted people will surely continue to be an inspiration to those who are still afraid to break free.

Freedom At My Reach

After my youth service, I returned to the university for my master's in analytical chemistry. As I did in my undergraduate days, I lived a life of freedom, managing to scrape through the required examinations and carried on waiting for my opportunity to get rich.

My siblings offered to sponsor me to continue to Ph.D. but by then I had concluded that I could not make it rich where I was and so I was determined to go abroad. I worked briefly for a food manufacturing company but resigned one day when the company owner asked me to do a job I thought was beneath my grade. I was so full of arrogance and pride! One of my closest friends then gave me an invitation to join him in another African country and I gladly took the opportunity.

I believe leaving my country of birth and the immediate vicinity of my relatives was very instrumental in breaking out of my spiritual darkness but the journey still took another eleven years. The country I relocated to was a fun-loving country and I continued my reckless and irresponsible lifestyle. I paraded myself as a

Muslim by going to the mosque there on Fridays but there was nothing of a relationship with God.

I met and married my wife from the new country and after I left Africa to study and subsequently settle in the United Kingdom. My wife chose to marry me as a Muslim and notwithstanding the bad behaviour she was aware of. I don't know what she saw in me because honestly, I would not have married someone like me if I was in her shoes. I suppose that is love or more precisely God's plan.

My family gave consent to the marriage with the condition that my wife converted to Islam. She was given a Muslim name and a new birth certificate the same year when we visited my parents. But we both knew that was just ceremonial as I had no intention of making her practice Islam. Neither did my wife express any expectation of me becoming a Christian but I think she may have been praying about it. We named our first daughter in the Islamic way and I gave her my mother's name.

I thank God for sparing my life as I put myself in dangerous situations so many times in that country. My friends still joke that the police knew my car very well. There was a particular incident I remember when driving home from a night out with a friend and I just decided to face an oncoming vehicle. Thank God the friend had the sense to swerve the steering away from a collision. I still don't know what was going through my head at that time.

Meanwhile, my yearly or twice yearly visions of Jesus' second coming continued whilst I was in this country. As usual, I would be sad for a few days or so and then carry on.

Moving to the UK did not initially change anything in terms of my faith in God. I, however, did not attend the mosque on Fridays as I used to do. This was probably due to my very busy schedule then as I was studying full time and working many hours for the first few years. My bad behaviour also reduced mostly due to the impact of law enforcement agents in the country. I paid a lot of traffic fines and even lost my driver's licence for a year due to various driving offences. I went through a change of career to become a care professional and this meant that I had to be careful not to get a criminal conviction.

My very first real experience of coming into a church environment was through my work as a support worker. I was given a shift supporting Isaac, a young adult with learning disabilities to go to church on Sundays.

I did this for about a year and so became a regular attendee at the church. To me, it was just an easy job to make money but I couldn't help but be impacted by the experience. I also believe I started making some sense of Christianity from listening to the weekly sermons.

I was impressed by this disabled young adult who found every aspect of his daily living hard but was always excited to go to church. That was one day of the week when he would be immaculately and smartly dressed. He would be very sad and upset if he missed church for any reason. I met his mother who was equally passionate about God and she let me know how important it was for her son to go to church.

And then the congregation! They were just awesome friendly people who showed their love to me in every possible way they could. The congregation was culturally diverse; very welcoming and so Isaac and I were fully included in all the church activities. This congregation invited me and my family to a weekend retreat which was perhaps the first real sense of hospitality we had in the United Kingdom.

Apart from attending church for work as described above, I started to also attend church for special occasions such as Christmas or Easter services. Our family moved home to a new area a few years later and we got to meet a new set of friends who were passionate about their church and started inviting us to the weekly service. Our children first, then my wife and later on I started to also attend the church.

Decision Time

As my attendance started to become regular in the church I began taking in some of the teachings. Within a few months, I became a regular member and even started attending Church in the Home. Then there came an opportunity to formally accept Jesus Christ as my Lord and Saviour.

It was my first trip back to my wife's country and I travelled with her and my two daughters. My wife was pregnant with our third child and one of our plans for the trip was to mark my fortieth birthday. Our family was already receiving the blessings of my new life in Christ and we were all in very good spirits for the trip.

I answered the Altar Call[9] to receive Jesus Christ as my personal Lord and Saviour in a church service in my wife's country on the Sunday before my 40th birthday. The thought I remembered clearly when I heard the altar call was 'a fool at forty is a fool forever'. I realised I knew the truth and for some reason, I was failing to take full hold of it. So when the call was made I stood up and took the walk to the front to pray and receive my gift of salvation.

I was among a group of people that prayed to accept Jesus Christ into our lives that day. The church took us to a room and gave us some guidance on how to continue our new life in Christ. I was relieved to have finally made the decision but apart from that, I did not experience any immediate change. At that time I still struggled with all the usual vices including the use of alcohol and smoking. So my life did not yet reflect my new faith in Christ. But God was already powerfully intervening in my life and we experienced what can only be described as a miracle on our return journey.

Our journey back was delayed because of a general problem with ash clouds in the atmosphere, which meant all flights were grounded for many days. My pregnant wife then developed some complications and experienced a lot of bleeding. We went to a private hospital where we were told that even if we used all the money in our credit card to pay for treatment, it would not resolve the problem and we might still need to pay more. We decided not to spend the money and to return to the UK where at least the treatment would be free. We assumed the pregnancy was already lost.

We were pleasantly surprised and grateful to God when we discovered the pregnancy was still intact on our arrival back in the United Kingdom. I believed God answered our prayers and gave us a miracle son despite all the loss of blood and despite the negative medical opinion.

The First Test Of Faith

My first real test of faith came shortly after my formal decision to follow Jesus. My sister-in-law was diagnosed with cancer in the same year and died a few months later. I travelled to the US to commiserate with my older brother. Now my brother is a devout Muslim and so he calls everyone in his household to prayer as my father used to do. The choice I had was either to pretend I was a Muslim and follow him in the doctrinal prayers five times a day or I had to tell him I was no longer a Muslim.

That decision is one of the toughest I have had to make since I accepted Jesus as my Lord and Saviour. I already knew by then that I could not live a lie as a follower of Christ. But I was there to comfort and encourage my older brother who was devastated over the loss of his wife and overwhelmed with the prospect of raising his four children alone. The dilemma was if I told my brother about my new faith in Christ, to him it would be like he had lost two close members of his family, his wife, and his brother. But if I didn't tell him, then I would have to pretend and lie that I was a Muslim throughout my stay with him. As I went to bed that first night I prayed to God to help me to be sure I have made the right decision as a lot was at stake.

How did God show up again? You guess right, in a dream! That same night I had the vision of Jesus Christ's second coming again in a dream. The start of the dream was similar to all the other twenty or so times before it. I realised it was happening, but this time I looked up to the sky in joyful anticipation instead of the usual fear, despair, sadness, desperation, helplessness, and hopelessness that I used to feel.

I looked up and there again was Jesus descending on his white horse in all his glory with the host of angels. Again the brilliance and awesomeness of the entourage was not something I could stand looking at so I fell facedown and then there was quietness. But instead of the usual fear, sadness, and expectation of condemnation, there was the excitement and joy that I am in Him. After a while, I felt Jesus was right behind me, and then he gently tapped me on the shoulder. I looked up and I saw him beckon to me with his hand as if to say 'come with me'. Then I woke up.

That was the second to last time I had the vision of Jesus' second coming. The last time was a couple of years after I accepted Christ as my Lord and Saviour. In the last dream I started jubilating immediately I thought the sky was going to open up to reveal Jesus descending. I was eagerly awaiting Jesus Christ to descend. But this time I got the timing wrong and the second coming did not happen. My interpretation of this last dream is that this showed the state of my faith that I was now fully in Christ and that I am confident that I shall be rejoicing when Christ returns.

The dream I had was enough to give me the courage to speak to my older brother about my new faith in Jesus Christ. To be fair he took the news much better than I expected. He listened to my explanations of my dreams and visions, and he asked me a few questions to check I wasn't losing my mind. He then warned me sternly not to let our parents know about it, something I had no intention of doing.

As if that was not the same fear that kept me from accessing my gift of salvation for fifteen years! I honestly believed at that time that my parents knowing about me becoming a Christian could kill them with sorrow or embarrassment.

But my God is always amazing! The person who told my parents about my new faith was a born again Christian wife of an old Muslim family friend that I didn't even have contact with. I found out that this woman after going on a mountain to pray went to my parents and told them she saw that I had become a Christian. That was it; I didn't need to tell my parents the supposedly bad news!

The second family member I told about my faith in Christ was my older sister as I felt she was going to be more liberal compared to other members of the family. She also took the news well but told me I had made the wrong decision and that she would be praying that I return to my senses. The fact that I lived in a different country away from all of my relatives meant that I was able to get involved in church life and partake in different opportunities to grow in my faith without the constant reminder of their disapproval.

Unlike my father, a few other family members have been antagonistic. At least one person openly blamed my wife as the cause, while another alluded that I may be experiencing a mental health breakdown. Another interrogated me on my conversion journey to find out if I was hoodwinked or placed under a spell! Most others will not even acknowledge my conversion or allow a discussion about faith and few told me they are actively praying for me to come back to Islam. I am praying for them too!

The New Life In Christ

The Bible makes it clear that people who have committed their lives to Jesus Christ will become a new creation. 2 Corinthians 5:17 states 'Therefore, if anyone is in Christ, the new creation has come: The old has gone, the new is here!' It is therefore important that any of us who claims to be a follower of Jesus must be able to look back to when we made the decision and how we have improved over time. I like to use two scriptural yardsticks as a measure of that new life in Christ.

The first is the use of what is known as the fruit of the Holy Spirit. Galatians 5:22 lists the fruit of the Holy Spirit as love, joy, peace, forbearance, kindness, goodness, faithfulness, gentleness, and self-control. But before you choose which the characteristics you may have improved, it is important to note the singular use of 'fruit' in the scripture. This means that everyone who has been made alive in Christ must exhibit personal growth in all the listed nine characteristics. I hope I have increased in these in the last ten years of following Jesus.

The second yardstick of growth and perhaps a more difficult one is what is described by Jesus in the Sermon on the Mount which is also referred to as the beatitudes (Matthew 5:1-12). Jesus used this sermon to list nine characteristics that predict specific blessings on his followers but these characteristics are not what you will normally expect. Jesus proclaimed specific blessings on his followers who are poor in spirit, those who mourn, the meek, those who hunger and thirst for righteousness, the merciful, the pure in heart, the peacemakers, those who are persecuted because of righteousness, and those who are insulted, persecuted and falsely accused because of Jesus.

I believe this second measure of growth is very crucial, because whilst we can be blinded as to how far we have grown in the fruit of the spirit, we cannot fail to realise when we are growing in the beatitude because of the insult, accusation, and persecution that will come as part of that growth. I need to reflect if the way I now do things is different from the way of the world and if I am growing stronger in facing the persecutory consequences of taking that position of righteousness. That is the only time I can rejoice and be glad because then I am sure that I have a great reward in heaven.

I can use the above two yardsticks to reflect on ten years of my new life in Christ, which by my account has been a huge transformation in my life and that of my immediate family, for the better. There are lots of things I can use to compare my life before and after accepting Jesus into my life but I will limit myself to a few main ones. The first was my giving up smoking a year after I accepted Jesus as my Lord and Saviour. Before then I had smoked every day for about twenty-five years.

I had not even made one single attempt to stop until I made the decision whilst praying on my second birthday after becoming born again. That was it, the chain was broken straight away and I never smoked again. My sleep and my mental health did not suffer as a result but only got better, praise God!

Apart from the smoking addiction, Jesus also delivered me from all the other vices that used to plague my life such as alcohol abuse and other reckless and risky behaviours. I am growing to be a more responsible family man and devoted to making up for lost time with my wife and children.

There has been a complete turnaround in my rebellion to God and all authorities. People find it hard to believe that this is the same Gaddaffi they knew previously. I am now fully submissive to God, I always seek what He wants me to do and I am determined to obey His commands no matter the cost. I am convinced that my choice to obey God's command is not borne out of fear but in the worship of the God who came to die for my sins so that I can have eternal life with Him. I pray daily for God to give me the spirit of humility so that I can respect and obey those in authority as long as it is not against God's commandments.

I believe I have grown a lot in recognising sinful behaviours and sinful thoughts in my life and I feel Godly sorrow anytime I realised I am walking into a sinful situation. This has helped me to cry out to God for forgiveness and help to overcome sins as they are revealed to me. I notice nowadays that minor infractions are magnified to me straight away so I can quickly seek God's help to kill the sinful thought before it develops further. This is the work of the Holy Spirit who dwells within me.

The change I loved most is my ability to hear God speak to me in many different ways which is fantastic. Of course, I need to keep working on waiting and listening more to God instead of taking matters into my own hands sometimes out of impatience. I enjoy spending time in prayer with God and I feel a closer relationship with the Holy Spirit and this is getting better by the day.

Apart from God himself, the credit for my spiritual growth can only be attributed to the church I attend. This is the only church I have attended as a member so I cannot say I have experiences of other congregations, but I have visited a few churches and have heard stories of what happens in other places.

I am very grateful to God that the first church I was attached to happens to be a great one. The church is a true, Bible-believing, teaching and acting church and both the leadership and the congregation try their best to obey God in everything they do. It is focused on developing personal character and leadership and every member is allowed to grow at their own pace. As for me, I had spent the first forty years of my life preparing for this new life so I have a lot to catch up and I can't afford to waste any more time.

Final Conclusion

Now that you have read my father's story and what is known of mine so far, what do you think? Do any of the accounts resonate with you or members of your family? Do you have any questions that are still unanswered? Do you feel in need to talk to someone about your thoughts?

Psychologists have proven through research that children have an intrinsic longing to be seen, approved, and accepted by their earthly fathers. We cry to hear the words 'I love you and I am very proud of you' from our fathers. This longing for our father's love and acceptance persists regardless of how successful we may be in areas of our lives such as in our jobs, relationships, marriage, and so on. We long for our father's love whoever we are.

There is also a universal truth that all our physical traits come to us from our parents and as we grow in wisdom we come to realise that many of our personality traits also come from our earthly parents. May I invite you to spend some time to reflect on those characteristics that you may have inherited from your parents? I am sure you will be surprised at how you are prone to making the same mistakes and errors of judgement that they did.

The good news is that there is a perfect Father who longs to be in a perfect relationship with us. We already have His love and affection and he is just waiting to shower us with His blessings. The perfect Father has offered us an opportunity to become part of his genealogy and he did this by sending his one and only son Jesus Christ to come down to us and directly lead us to the Father.

There is an opportunity for all of us to choose to belong to the holy and eternal family tree instead of the earthly sinful and corrupt genealogy of our parents. As stated in John 1:12 'to all who believed in his name, he gave the right to become children of God'. Jesus can grant us Spiritual and Godly DNA because he came down from heaven as a man, he lived the obedient life that God required us to live which we fail to do, he died the death that is due to us because of our sins, and then he rose back to life on the third day to prove he can also raise us on the last day.

My aim in writing this memoir is for you to know that you can also be free and that it is your personal choice. Many people follow their parent's beliefs or lack of belief in God, but each person will have to independently bear the cost of their decision. You owe it to yourself for the sake of eternity, to know and be sure of your eternal destination.

I hope you know that heaven is waiting for you. I hope you know of Jesus who came down from heaven to bear the cost of your sins and suffered, died and rose for you so that you can have eternal life. It is not too late if you are still not sure or assured of your salvation through Jesus Christ. Would you open your heart and pray to God to show himself to you through the means that will make sense to you so that you can be sure? You may also want to speak to someone that you know is a follower of Christ who can guide you and pray with you.

If you are like me and you are assured of your place in heaven, praise God! Keep seeking the Lord, keep spending time in his presence, and getting to know more of him. Accept and rejoice in the privilege of being able to have direct access to God who can do all things. You should live your new life in Christ and in freedom, which he purchased for you with his blood. You should look up to Jesus daily and do things the way he showed us by his life on earth. Jesus also left you his Holy Spirit to lead, guide, and empower you to obey his commands daily. Be reassured that as long as you keep your eyes on Jesus, you remain saved and guaranteed eternal life.

Please do not neglect your on-going work in praying and interceding for the world so that others may also enjoy the blessing of everlasting life with Jesus. Do not give up on anyone until they breathe their last, then move on praying and interceding for others. Let Jesus come and find us fighting for the souls of our loved ones!

GLOSSARY

1 Compound name – This is a name given to an area where descendants from a particular lineage lived. The name will usually reflect the occupation or religious beliefs of the people.

2 Born again - A born-again Christian is someone who has repented of their sins and turned to Christ for their salvation, and as a result, has become part of God's family forever.

3 Church in the Home – (Also known as a house, home, or cell church) is a label used to describe a group of Christians who regularly gather for worship in private homes. The group may be part of a larger Christian body.

4 Night Vigil - a period of keeping awake and praying during the time usually spent asleep.

5 Baal / Asherah (Prophets of) - an ancient Semitic goddess, worshiped by the Phoenicians and Canaanites. The Prophets were the priests of the Goddess temple.

6 Spirit – The Holy Spirit is the third person in the Trinity (which is God the Father, God the Son, and God the Holy Spirit). Praying in the Spirit means a prayer with unintelligible words and groans, also sometimes referred to as praying in tongues.

7 Messiah - The promised deliverer of the Jewish nation prophesied in the Hebrew Bible, a leader regarded as the saviour of a particular country or people.

8 Anti-Christ - is someone recognized as fulfilling the Biblical prophecies about one who will oppose Christ and substitute himself in Christ's place, a personal opponent of Christ expected to appear before the end of the world.

9 Altar Call - calling people forward after an evangelistic sermon to make a public confession of faith in Christ.

Printed in Great Britain
by Amazon

59722814R00086